The
Vanishing Virginian

BY

REBECCA YANCEY WILLIAMS

With an Introduction by
Douglas Southall Freeman

New York · 1940

E. P. DUTTON & COMPANY, INC.

FOR MARTIN

INTRODUCTION

By Douglas Southall Freeman

THE lightness and the laughter of this book must not be marred by heavy-handed authentication. It is not necessary. Within twenty pages after the introduction of "Cap'n Bob" Yancey, he emerges so clearly that one knows him to be a real person. From the time Mr. Yancey escapes a quarrel over his comment on his wife's efforts to reduce, every male reader will be satisfied that the outspoken husband is a man to be studied, to be admired and, within the limits of individual prowess or prudence, to be emulated. Thence onward to the exquisite end, the reader will be so much interested in the Yancey household, servants and all, that he would turn wrathfully on the antiquarian who chirped, "It's all true." When the Captain fairly snorts on every page, what need was there for his daughter to sharpen his high words? Besides, if she had, what difference would it make? It is as a literary and not as an historical portrayal that this book should have, I think, the same delighted welcome that was given Clarence Day's *Life with Father,* to which it presents a most charming contrast in locale and in outlook.

As an incidental remark, then, and not as a formal introduction, it may be said that all the solemn records square with Mrs. Williams' fascinating sketch of the background. In at least one instance, other testimony shows her conservative in statement. She says that when General Jubal A. Early was dug from the debris, after the collapse of the building in which he had his office, the first call of the old sol dier was for a julep. My Father, who was in the army of rescuers, always insisted that Early's first words were, "U-h-h, I didn't know there were that many bricks between me and hell."

What Mrs. Williams portrays of the spirit of Bedford and of Lynchburg fits in with her revelatory remark, "Looking back, it seems to me that all of my childhood was entangled with the past." Everything was so entangled. George W. Bagby, in *The Old Virginia Gentleman,* idealized the Bedford plantation Avenol as he remembered it "befo' the war." Mrs. Williams' memory of her Grandma Yancey's Rothsay in the same county does not go back, I should guess, much beyond 1910; but one is puzzled to say whether there is more of difference or of similarity between Rothsay and Avenol. The calm green permanence of the Peaks of Otter in that blessed country spares men the waste and the blindness of hurry. Roads wind caressingly; even the streams flow slowly.

Yesterday and the day before, in Robert Yancey's time—and in Becky's too—were tied together in

Lynchburg almost as closely as in Bedford. Old men lived under the hills that young persons climbed. General Early, who had his home near the head of Main Street, died in 1894. I remember him dimly as a glowering old man, fiercely chewing tobacco, who was notorious, our nurses would have us remember, for eating a bad little boy every morning at breakfast. Of course we shunned him, but our fathers did not. When he hobbled down to the Arlington Hotel in the morning, he might snarl and swear. Veterans would listen respectfully and never would answer back. Had he not saved the city at the time of Hunter's Raid? Was he not the embodiment of the Confederacy, to his last hour unparoled and unreconstructed, a Lieutenant-General in the Army of Northern Virginia?

Senator John W. Daniel, who had served on Early's staff, outlived his chief about sixteen years and in much the same manner governed Lynchburg for the vanished Confederacy. From his verdict on moot historical questions, none dared appeal. No Confederate monument could be accounted rightly unveiled or duly dedicated without an oration by him in the grand manner. Reunions and the burial of distinguished soldiers were the great events in the life of the city.

Robert Yancey had been too young and his Father too old to fight, yet in a day when a good rec-

ord as a Confederate soldier was the first credential
of a candidate for any office of profit or of honor,
Bob Yancey could not be beaten for renomination as
Commonwealth's Attorney. It was an immense trib-
ute to his popularity, but no less was it an indication
that times were changing and that silent younger
men were to have their day. Almost as much evidence of change was to be seen in the election and
re-election of a prosecutor who was not a Confederate veteran as there was in the fact that one after another of the chewing-tobacco factories in Lynchburg
closed down. A nervous generation was disdaining
the reflective quid and was demanding cigarettes.
Becky Williams summarizes all this in her own way
when she maintains that her Father represented the
Old South, that her Mother exemplified the mid-
Victorian in Virginia, and that the seven children
were "hard-crusted moderns" who "belonged," as
she says, "to the age when Virginia was just beginning to become Americanized."

Although the lights cross on Mr. Yancey, his wife
is not left in vague shadow. She was twenty years
younger than her husband, and if he is unique she is
typical without loss of individuality. The resigna-
tion, not to say the calmness, with which many another woman of her day accepted the temperamental
peculiarities of a husband was outward only. Somewhat dearly, when the doors were closed, the gentle-

man would have to pay for violent words or un-
gracious acts, and if he dared make a stand, he had
to retreat quickly before a barrage of tears. A wife of
the eighteen-nineties would cry as torrentially over
her husband's shortcomings as her daughter weeps
now over the misadventures of the hero of a movie.
Mrs. Yancey did not cry often, but, it seems to me,
she held her own pretty well against all comers. Nor
was an occasional "moratorium," as Becky calls it, or
the reading of a book, or a long discourse on genealogy a mere escape device. She found time to publish
in 1935 a sizeable volume *Lynchburg and Its Neighbors,* to which she added some scores of genealogies.
Although she often was silenced by voluble husband
and by chattering children, she of all the Yanceys—
who knows?—may have the last word.

Surprisingly few Virginians born since 1850 have
sought to say the last word about their neighbors or
about themselves in autobiographies. Half-a-dozen
of the Confederate Generals, some of the Colonels
and many of the junior officers and privates wrote of
the war; but, curiously enough, the only two major
narratives in the first person since silence fell on the
camps, have been those of distinguished Negroes—
Booker Washington and Robert Moton. When
newspapers printed since about 1885 have fallen to
dust, as most of them will within fifty years, poster-
ity will know little of the life of the Virginians of

the closing decades of the nineteenth century. The only book I have known, prior to this, that presented the Virginia scene at its best from the end of reconstruction to about 1910, is John Stewart Bryan's *Joseph Bryan,* and that work, most unfortunately, was printed exclusively for private circulation. Where Mr. Bryan ends, Mrs. Williams takes up. She presents actors who had other interests on a different stage, but the setting is as surely Virginian. Is it exclusively, provincially Virginian? I do not think so. As Mrs. Williams has presented her Father in the twenty sketches that follow, Robert Yancey seems to have the vitality a Fielding would have given him. I feel the better reconciled to life for having heard him swear.

CONTENTS

THE VANISHING VIRGINIAN

CHAPTER I

My Mother Tries to Reduce

vvvvv

FATHER lived in Virginia. I suppose he was what
is called a small-town politician, for he was Commonwealth's Attorney of Lynchburg for thirty-five
years, and Lynchburg, having only forty thousand
inhabitants, is certainly a small. town. Moreover,
Lynchburg is a typical Virginia small town, since it
has never had very much influx from the outside
world. Almost every family that lives there now has
lived thereabout for at least a hundred and fifty
years. One can't keep skeletons locked away in such
a place, and this fact emboldens me to write Father's
unconventional story.

My father's father had been Commonwealth's Attorney of Lynchburg before him. His family had
been among the founders and important citizens of
the town since its beginning. So my father took it

for granted that heredity had been intensified in him and that he, in his day, was Lynchburg's most important citizen. This was all settled. It was something he never had to worry about, and it gave him full liberty to behave as he pleased. My mother said he acted as if he thought his office was hereditary and that he was the King of Lynchburg.

My mother never took her position quite so much for granted. My mother's mother was what was known as "a beauty." My mother was also considered a beauty. As all of mother's sisters were lovely to look at, and all her brothers wonderfully handsome, my mother used to go through some quite transparent motions of pretending not to understand *why* the children of her brothers and sisters were not so beautiful as her own children. This was very comical, for not one of us was anything above the average. But Mother thought we were. And this faculty of hers gave her a tremendous feeling of superiority over her own brothers and sisters. Nevertheless, she did not have that natural sense of being a privileged person that Father had.

My mother's mother was beautiful to the day she died. She had all of the soft feminine loveliness which was the flower of the Victorian era. Mother had all of that too. But none of her daughters had any of it. We were raised up in the school of cold

18

realism, and this took away whatever femininity we might have possessed.

My mother always made much of the fact that her great-great-great-grandfather was the third President of the College of William and Mary, Rector of Bruton Parish Church, "ordained by the Bishop of London and sent to Williamsburg as head of the Church of England in America." This was to offset the fact that my father felt that he *was* Lynchburg and didn't give a damn if nobody agreed with him. His absolute security in this feeling cramped Mother's style more than a little.

Of course Mother's people were every bit as nice as Father's. But Mother's father was from Winchester. While everyone knows that Winchester is in Virginia and is quite a charming old town, still my mother's father had not been born in the place where he lived. That offended an English sensibility which still clings to Virginians. I myself do not know how to explain this sensibility—unless the general idea is that if a person amounted to anything where he came from he never would have left there. But whatever the explanation, I do know that my mother was always apologetic because her father had not been born in Lynchburg.

Some of Grandmother's relatives had not reflected any particular credit upon "the Rector of Bruton

Parish Church and the head of the Church of England in America." So Mother was subconsciously bothered about that too.

Plenty of my father's relations had not shed any particular distinction upon his family traditions either. He did not require that all his family connections should be rich and famous. He never tried to suppress the fact that they were not. Such things did not worry Father in the least. He had an instinctive sense of superiority which nothing could blast.

My mother was cursed with the inherited name of Rosa. Besides that, she had a brilliant color, and the combination polished her off for life. This was because when she was a small tot, Grandfather had started calling her "Rosebud." The name always stuck to Mother and, after the advent of seven children, it seemed very ridiculous. My mother used to say wistfully, "I look more like a rose*bush* now."

None of us children thought our mother was anything but as pleasingly plump as a mother should be. But one day my Aunt Tucker expressed the opinion that Mother weighed more than she herself did. They were both young matrons under thirty-five. They both had new babies, and it is perfectly natural for young matrons with new babies to be a little on the plump side. But when Aunt Tucker made this remark, my mother looked surprised and hurt. She looked as if she were imagining herself, for the first time, as others saw her. As well as I remember, they never did settle the matter with scales. But the argument which resulted from my aunt's remark was what started Mother on her reducing program. She tried various methods.

In the summer we always went to Bedford County to stay with my father's mother. She was Grand*ma*. She lived about twelve miles out from Lynchburg in a sweet old place which had been the summer home of my father's family. Behind Grandma's house there was quite a long lane which led past the overseer's house, past the wells, the hen houses, the cornhouses, the icehouse, and so on to the barn.

My mother did nothing about her argument with Aunt Tucker as long as we were in town. But she evidently made up her mind to show her a thing or two, for as soon as we arrived in the country she started on reducing. At first she tried to be very secretive about it. She conceived the idea of taking an early morning sprint up the lane to the barn and back before any of the family was awake. But she reckoned without us children. We were up at daylight as usual. We were building sand houses in the side yard by way of entertaining ourselves until breakfast time. When we saw Mother slink through the side gate and go dog-trotting up the lane, we all rushed forward with a wild war whoop and fell in step behind her.

At last she was doing something in which we could take part! We were delighted. So the whole family—minus my father—sallied forth for several mornings.

But this didn't last long. It was too strenuous for Mother. It made her ache all day. Also, she didn't like the way we children, running fleetly behind her, laughed at the way she shook all over. It hurt her vanity. So she tried horseback riding.

Father had some very good horses. There was Mohamet, Mother's riding horse, which she had not ridden since her fourth child was born. Then there was Lena, my father's horse; and there was old Charles, who was broad and white and gentle. My brother Bob had a Texas pony branded with a large S, and he would throw you if he got half a chance. There was another grey horse which I remember as a distinct personality. Her name was originally Nannie. But no amount of feeding would ever fatten her. She always looked lank and rawboned, so my father rechristened her "Rozinante" and let it go at that. The colored people around the farm, who were not initiated into the mysteries of *Don Quixote,* thought that Father had merely added a prefix to "Nannie" in compliment to Mother, so they called the grey horse "Rosa-Nannie." This seemed quite right and proper to them, for the best riding horse of all was named "Lucy," for Grandma.

At any rate, there were enough horses on the place to mount anyone who felt inclined to ride, and everyone who was old enough to stay in a saddle. And it was a big thrill for us children that Mother was joining in a sport we loved.

Our great agility must have been hard for Mother to bear. While her horse was being led around to the block and held for her, we were on ours in a jiffy. We began by jumping over all the benches in the yard and galloping off full tilt. But we did not forget Mother. We would race back to her three or four times in every mile to see if she was still on. We rode astride, dressed in anything we happened to be wearing, and none of the girls was at all abashed if her little ruffled pants chanced to show. However, Mother was raised in the Victorian school. Riding was a ceremony with her. It was very hot weather, but she rode a sidesaddle and was dressed in a full, long habit and a derby hat. The way she held up her skirts as she came from the front door when her horse was brought up never failed to impress me as being very elegant. But I wondered how she could ride in so many clothes. She didn't very long.

Grandma's place in the country was three miles from Forest Depot. Father commuted to Lynchburg by train and he had to drive to and from the station in a buggy. One Friday, he came driving in from the station just as we were returning from our afternoon canter. Down the road clattered five excited youngsters, each yelling like a wild Indian and urging his horse forward in the effort to be the first to see if Father had brought us anything from town. At the tail end of the procession came Mother, bouncing violently along on Mohamet. Mohamet was a spirited horse in spite of his eight years. The thrill of the race was in his blood and Mother was having a desperate time trying to hold him and to keep herself and her hat on, all at the same time. She did not look at all happy, and Mohamet didn't seem to like it either. It must have been a funny sight, for my father burst out laughing as he helped Mother down.

"Well, well," he said, "—so the mountain did come to Mohamet."

This was the last time Mother ever got on a horse. But that remark cost my father money, for Mother next tried to reduce by taking Kissingen and Vichy water.

I do not know if these fascinating drugs are still on the market but, when I was a child, they were sold in the drugstores of Lynchburg in the shape of crystal salts put up in beautiful bottles. I remember the lovely bottles especially, and the way the salts fizzed up when you added water to them. It was great fun for all of us children to watch the salts fizz.

Mother really did lose weight when she took the stuff, too. And she was so pleased that she called upon all of us to admire the way her waistline had melted. We were duly admiring, and even impressed by the amount of power in those small crystals.

But when the bill from the drugstore came my mother was bowled over. She was ashamed to show it to Father, so she hid it in her chest of drawers. Sometimes when I was rummaging around for candy or trying to find some clothes with which to "play ladies," I used to see the bill tucked away in Mother's bureau. Then one day there were two of the bills—then in course of time three—and four—carefully hidden in Mother's clothes.

My poor lovely mother! With seven little explorers always on hand, she never had any privacy. In church, even today, at the beginning of that beautiful and stately prayer, "Almighty God, to whom all hearts are open, all desires known and from whom no secrets are hid," I pause to reflect how truly this also applies to a family of young children.

When finally there was quite a collection of bills in Mother's bureau, and some very uncomplimentary letters had been added to the lot, she could not stand the strain any longer. She handed the bills to my father and he hit the ceiling.

"Good God! What in the hell is this?" he asked.

Mother explained that it was because he had called her a mountain. She shed a few pretty tears and she told him it was all his fault.

It took a lot more explaining yet to quiet Father's purple oaths. But my mother was so sweet; and she had such a gentle voice that at last, having no competition, Father wore out his rage. However, when he wrote the check he told my mother she would have to control her appetite. He said my mother would have to make up her mind to stop eating so much. He would just be damned if he would pay to fatten her up and then pay to unfatten her.

Mother was so delighted to get her bills paid that she did not remind Father of the fact that she never ate half so much as he did. It was painful to any Victorian lady to be accused of having a large appetite. But Mother let that pass. Still, she never tried to reduce again. The struggle was too great for her. And she always retained her curves. Regardless of any remark my aunt might make, my mother knew that she was prettier than any of her sisters. In that certain knowledge my mother was always secure. She really was not mountainous at all. She could afford a few curves, she said.

CHAPTER II

Pastoral Pictures

vvvv

ALTHOUGH the place in Bedford County had originally been only Grandma's summer home, she had not returned to Lynchburg since the War Between the States. When the war came she and Grandpa had moved to the farm in Bedford, and they had given the house in Lynchburg to be used as a hospital for Confederate soldiers. Their eldest son, Henry, was killed at the Battle of Spotsylvania Courthouse and, after Grandpa's death, Grandma said she wanted to stay in the country. She said all of her old friends were dead and everything was so changed in Lynchburg that she did not ever want to see the town again. But the real reason was that Grandma liked the country better than town. She enjoyed the quiet austerity of the winters and our visits in the summer brought her plenty of confusion and excitement to round out her year.

My mother was twenty years younger than Father, and when some of us children were as old as ten and twelve she was still a rather young person. Father always liked people of all ages, and Mother was incurably romantic to the end of her days, and so they both loved to have their young, unmarried friends come up to Bedford in the summer.

Father's and Mother's young guests were irresistible to Grandma, and when she heard their happy laughing voices in the house, down she would come and join them. And if there was a game of croquet going on in the yard Grandma never failed to appear; for she, in her day, had been quite good at that game. So she would have her chair pulled up to one of the groups of charming young creatures watching the croquet, and she would enter into their enthusiastic chitchat. Indeed, the young ladies made a picture pretty enough to be irresistible to anyone, with their long ruffled skirts, their pink and blue ribbon sashes and their high wavy pompadours. The young men seemed as enchanted with them as was Grandma, and they all welcomed Grandma into their conversation, for she was exceedingly witty and entertaining.

Our whole family was sorry when one of Father's and Mother's house parties was over; but the blow of departure was softened by a very special treat which always came at the end. This was a trip to spend the night on the top of the Peaks of Otter and, each year, one of us children was allowed to go along with the party.

About a hundred years ago, John Randolph had said that no man could ever be an atheist who had seen the glorious sight of sunrise from the top of the Peaks of Otter. As long as he lived, John Randolph would come once a year to watch the sunrise from the Peaks, and it became a Bedford County custom to do likewise.

A very crude log house on top of the mountain was kept as a hotel for overnight parties. There was a huge room on the first floor which was used as a dining room and living room, and the upper floor was separated into two large dormitories—one for men and the other for women. It was great fun to spend the night up there, for you would find yourself in the next bed to someone whom you had not seen for years. However, it was not at all democratic. The cabin on the mountain was used only by those who belonged to the cult of old Bedford County traditions. To go there was somewhat like staying in an exclusive club, even though the custom, presumably, was begun as a gesture against atheism. If any strangers inadvertently blew in, it was funny to see "our" women look down their noses at them.

After the sunrise every morning, a typical Virginia breakfast was served. Virginia ham, fried apples, scrambled eggs, batter bread and steaming hot coffee were passed around the great table, while the men sat discussing politics and the women exchanged gossip and vital statistics. And, naturally, the presence of strangers did interfere with this cozy ceremony.

The trip to the Peaks took all day from our house. Early in the morning our old colored servant, Uncle Jake, would have the carriages ready, and each one was fitted up with a large basket of lunch. Just outside of Bedford City was the stopping place where the horses were fed and watered; and here Mother would get out a huge tablecloth which was spread in a grove of trees near the road. Then the fried chicken, the sandwiches and the cakes and pies were unpacked and everyone fortified himself for the climb ahead. From there you could drive halfway up the mountain, but it was stiff pulling for the horses, and they always seemed glad when "halfway" was reached, for here they were put into the stables to rest until morning.

And now began the real thrill of going up—up under your own power; and it was ideal for house parties for it offered many a chance for a shy handclasp and sometimes even a bold upward yank by both hands. This was all very exciting to me when I went along on my first trip to the Peaks and I was expecting adventures, but I did not expect the kind of adventure we had.

When we arrived at the cabin on the top, our ladies immediately observed that we were not the only guests of the house. They got into a huddle and they began to whisper and to shake their heads. They did not know a single person in the other party. It consisted of three young couples, and apparently there was not a qualified chaperon among them. My mother did not like the looks of this, and she went to Father about it. But Father refused to concern himself. He said the mountain did not belong to him. What did Mother want to do? Start back to Forest and drive all night? Or should we all go down and sleep in the stables? Of course he had Mother there, for she did not wish to do either. And so after supper, instead of sitting around on the rocks and enjoying the delicious cold air and the clear moon-silvered sky until late at night, Mother and her friends decided to set an example. They retired to their sleeping quarters promptly at eleven o'clock.

But their example didn't bear fruit. Some of Mother's young ladies put their hair up in curlpapers. They sat around and talked. They got into their beds. But they did not put out the lights. Time passed. Every now and then one of Mother's friends would sit bolt upright in bed and wonder "when on earth those people were coming in."

More time passed. We all dozed off to sleep.

Suddenly a great commotion sounded all around us. There was wild screeching and running back and forth. We all sat bolt upright in our beds.

"Snakes! There's a rattlesnake in here!" one of "those people" was proclaiming, and she was unbarring the heavy door which separated our dormitory from the men's room. Three strange young men came bounding through the door. They were not actually undressed but they had taken off their shirts.

"Oh! Good heavens!" exclaimed Mother's friends, and they all slid under the covers; and those who had on curlpapers pulled the sheets up over their heads.

And there really was a large snake. It had draped itself around the headpost of a vacant bed and it had made its presence known just as one of "those people" had attempted to hang her coat there.

The three young men took off their shoes and, armed with these, they went after the snake, banging and whacking all over the room, with the three young girls screaming and running at their heels. And during all this tumult there was not so much as a sound from any of our men.

The snake was soon killed and thrown out of the window onto the rocks below. But then the three young men did not modestly retire. Instead, they sat on the vacant beds with their girl friends and they all exchanged snake stories and, in modern beach style, they made themselves very much at home.

My mother had never seen anything like this. She began to squirm. Here she was in the position of chaperon, and yet she was flat on her back in bed with the cover pulled up to her chin. She knew she ought to do something, but what she ought to do required that she be fully clothed and standing haughtily on her feet. At the very least she should be sitting in a chair, where she could draw herself up to a dignified posture. Since Mother could manage none of this, she packed all of her outraged dignity into her voice.

"Young ladies," said she, "if your friends have finished disposing of the snake, I think they should go to their own room." The young men hastily departed. There was a dense silence.

The next morning all of us dressed and went downstairs before the strangers were up; and Mother and her friends were in quite a huff. "Why didn't you come and kill that snake instead of allowing those strange men to prance all over our room?" Kate Randolph demanded, turning on Ned Hamner.

"I was not dressed—" he began, but Mother interrupted.

"It was your place to come," she declared, turning on Father.

"I was not dressed," he began, and then he broke into hearty laughter. "Women!" he chuckled. "I'll never understand them! You had rather have a rattlesnake in your room than a few harmless strangers!"

CHAPTER III

Family Stuff

vvvvv

MY GREAT-GRANDFATHER had bought his original tract of land in Bedford from Thomas Jefferson, who owned thousands of acres in the county, and who had built "Poplar Forest," a typical Jeffersonian home. Great-Grandfather, with his cousin, William Radford, had come to Bedford from New Kent County soon after the Revolution, and together they had purchased a beautiful stretch of country at the foot of the Blue Ridge Mountains. The loveliness of the view from their homes is enough to shake the very roots of one's soul.

My great-grandfather called his place "Rothsay," and he said he wanted to be buried there in sight of his mountains. So his grave is in the garden at the side of the house. He lived to a ripe old age and he died of acute indigestion after eating a large quantity of black-heart cherries. A cherry tree grew out of the middle of his grave, and though the colored people on the place raided all the other fruit trees, none of them ever touched a cherry on that one, which they called "Marse Joel's tree."

William Radford had just escaped being one of the casualties of the Revolution, for he had equipped a number of privateers to fight the British and had been captured and confined in the Tower of London. But through the influence of friends and relations in England, he was freed from the Tower and made his way to France, where Marie Antoinette assisted him to return to America. Ever an adventurous person, it was he who had persuaded his young cousin, my great-grandfather, to come with him to Bedford County.

Great-Grandfather built his home on the next plantation to Thomas Jefferson, and he and Jefferson were quite close friends. When Jefferson had to be absent from "Poplar Forest," Great-Grandfather was his official host, and for many years they kept up a voluminous correspondence on various political and agricultural subjects. My mother was always very proud of the friendship with Jefferson; she thought it gave Father's family an intellectual stamp. Father had his own reasons for being greatly amused at this.

My mother was never an intensive housekeeper, but when we first moved to the country in the summer or moved back to town in the fall, she got extremely energetic about what she called "getting the house straight."

It is true that Grandma kept her room in a mess. She would never let anyone clean it except Aunt Nancy, who had been her maid for many years and who did not dare to move one single thing without Grandma's permission. But Grandma herself could find anything in her room at a moment's notice. She had some bookshelves which were overflowing with books and old magazines and bundles of old letters. And from behind these she could bring forth lollipops and cans of tea cakes, or even balls of cord and a hammer and nails, if you happened to want them for something you were making. All winter, while we were in town, she saved paper dolls for us girls and she collected puzzles and clippings about odd facts of history and science for the boys. Grandma never threw away a thing. She had old shoe boxes full of Confederate bonds and money which we borrowed at times when we wished to play bank. But Grandma knew everything she had by name. When we borrowed her belongings we were required to account for them in her presence. And, when we brought them back, we had to check them in under Grandma's own sharp eyes, which had never needed the assistance of spectacles even for threading a needle.

Of course, Father did not care how Grandma's room was kept, and all of us children thought it was a wonderful place to visit. But once a year, for a few days after we arrived in the country, it worried Mother no end. Grandma would not let her get it "straight," and that was that.

One year, Mother made up her mind that something would have to be done about Grandma's room. Accordingly, she planned a lovely trip for Grandma. She arranged for Uncle Jake to drive her over to New London to spend the day at Bedford Alum Springs. Mother knew that Grandma had passed many happy seasons at Bedford Alum in her youth; so Grandma was to visit her old friends and have a grand time. My mother told Grandma that she had too few pleasures—she should go around and enjoy herself more before she grew too old. And although Grandma was then eighty-six years old, she fell for this—hook, line and sinker.

Soon after breakfast the next morning, then, Grandma left for New London. Uncle Jake drove her in the family carriage, with Aunt Nancy on the front seat by his side, and Grandma sat on the back seat in high spirits. She had a basket of small presents with her which she was taking to her various friends.

No sooner were they around the bend in the road than Mother got to work. She had three large barrels moved up to Grandma's room and these were soon filled with old magazines and many bundles of letters tied together with cord.

Next, Mother had Grandma's bookshelves scrubbed, and she arranged Grandma's books in neat, orderly rows. When all of this was done, Mother had Grandma's four windows washed and pretty new curtains hung at them. Then she looked around with a sigh of satisfaction: How pleased Grandma would be when she saw how sweet her room *could* look with a little attention!

After everything was finished, Mother had the three full barrels carried down to the lane by the well house, and to the collection was added a small hair-covered trunk, packed with papers, which Grandma had always kept under her bed. Then Mother struck a match to the pile of stuff herself, and she told all of us children that we could stay and enjoy the bonfire. We had a wonderful time the whole afternoon, poking the fire with long sticks.

When Grandma returned from New London late that day, she was in a gay mood. She had had a delightful day. Her eyes sparkled like a young girl's in spite of her eighty-six years. Always very small and erect, she tripped lightly up to her room. But she came down like an overcharged thunderbolt, calling:

"Robert, Robert, *what has* your wife done!"

There was quite a scene.

Mother had burned up all of Thomas Jefferson's letters to my great-grandfather, and some other very valuable old papers besides!

So, whenever Mother mentioned "The Friendship" with Thomas Jefferson, my father would laugh. He said she talked a lot about the facts, but she had destroyed all the evidence.

The little town of New London was about five miles from our place. Here also was old New London Academy, where Patrick Henry had made his famous speech in the Johnny Hook case; and Bedford Alum Springs, which had been a fashionable resort when Grandma was a young lady. The town of New London was thriving in 1750, and was quite a flourishing community at the time of the Revolution. One of the first United States armories was located there, and Joseph Martin, in his early *Gazetteer,* describes New London Academy as "a handsome and commodious Academy where a student may be prepared to enter any of the Colleges or Universities with credit."

Many of the buildings of the old town and academy had been burned down by General Hunter during the War Between the States and, at the time I remember it, New London was a very forlorn village. Still, it had that atmosphere which always clings to places rich in human experience. Forlorn though it was, New London was filled with an air of hovering spirits. It was as if each person who had loved the place had left there something of himself —something that spoke with an eloquent voice. And as we used to ride up the bumpy old stagecoach road, between tall rows of mock-orange trees, to picnic at Bedford Alum Springs, I was lost in a dream of the past.

The ramshackle and deserted old hotel at the Alum Springs was built in the shape of a semicircle, and there was a high and beautiful semicircle of boxwood in front, where the driveway had wound around. Summer houses were sprinkled all over the wide lawn, which was shaded by magnificent trees, and the remains of a lovely old garden straggled off to the side. The unkempt grass, here and there, was choked with bergamot which smelled delicious when you stepped upon it, and this stirred up poignant thoughts of a happy, gracious yesterday; but the thing that intrigued me most about New London was the cobbled stagecoach road itself. Grandma had in her stable an old green and gold family coach in which we used to play "Cinderella," and whenever we turned up the rocky stage road, I could always see Grandma's coach, new and shiny, bumping up the hill between the mock-orange trees, while the flowers on the bonnet of a young Grandma bobbed up and down with each jolt.

New London was almost a deserted town. Clapboard houses were falling to decay, and on the short stretch of road from New London Academy to Bedford Alum Springs there were some fine, sturdy old brick homes which had not been occupied for years. One of these places was called "Merry Oaks"; when it had been deserted, even the furniture was left behind. The furniture had never been disturbed because "Merry Oaks" was supposed to be haunted.

On picnics, we would go in to play on the jangly old harpsichord at "Merry Oaks," and we would dramatize "Goldilocks and the Three Bears" on the rickety chairs and beds. But this was early in the nineteen-hundreds, before the "antique" rage hit this country. I suppose all of these attractions to picnickers have long ago been carried away from the old place, for I have known "antique" enthusiasts to be guilty of depredations which we commonly associate only with the most underprivileged persons.

On all our picnics Elizabeth was the most bold and venturesome. She was the eldest of us and I never saw anyone with such superb self-confidence as she had. It was she who discovered at "Merry Oaks" that an old threshing machine in the decaying barn was inhabited by bees; and she suggested that we kill all the bees and get their honey.

I had no quarrel with any bees. I did not particularly want their honey. But all the others, especially the boys, thought it would be very exhilarating to have a fight with bees. They armed themselves with small branches from some saplings, and they found long poles which they rammed down into the cracks of the threshing machine so that the bees would come forth and do battle. When the bees swarmed out they flailed right and left with their saplings.

I was generally a cautious child, and I have always had great respect for my hide. So I climbed into the tallest tree I could find, where I settled myself as a mere spectator.

Elizabeth ordered the attacks. She would toss her golden curls like a long yellow banner and rush forward to the fray herself. This made the boys ashamed to retreat and determined not to yell when they got stung. All of them got stung a plenty, but the ground around the threshing machine was brown with bees when I came down from my roost. They got some honey, too, but they would not give me any. Elizabeth wouldn't let them, because she said I had not fought for it.

When we got home that evening the whole crowd, excepting myself, were covered with great bumps. They were no longer in heroic spirit and Mother had all she could do to quiet their complaints with wet soda. Elizabeth was the worst of all, because she had dead bees all tangled up in her long yellow hair. Some of them were not quite dead, for one stung my mother with its last gasp while she was trying to comb it out.

Mother was exhausted when Father got back from Lynchburg that night. She was very cross. She said she did not know why all her children were so pugnacious. She had sent us out with sufficient lunch for the day, and we did not need any honey. She did not see why we had to disturb those poor bees and rob them of their winter's food. All of her children were belligerent like my father's family. When she was a child none of her brothers or sisters would ever have thought of such a thing as battling with bees. Elizabeth was always getting the other children into trouble. She was a perfect Yancey in every way.

My father said Elizabeth had more courage and a damn sight better brain than any of us. Of course she was like the Yanceys.

And Mother said she would have him know that her family had brains and courage as well as his; but they were not so desperate for a place to show it off that they would go out and stir up a beehive.

CHAPTER IV

Black and White

∿∿∿

LOOKING back, it seems to me that all of my childhood was entangled with the past. Grandma had at her place some of the old colored servants who had remained with her from slavery times, and chief among these were Aunt Nancy and her husband, Uncle Jake. Aunt Nancy was long and lean, black as an ace of spades, and neat as a pin. She was head man, as far as we children were concerned. She was entirely respectful to Mother and "Old Miss," as she called Grandma, but she ruled us children and Uncle Jake with a rod of iron.

Mother always referred to Uncle Jake and Aunt Nancy as the Darby and Joan of the African race. She said their devotion to each other was a poem. However, all of us children understood perfectly that the secret of their married bliss lay in the fact that Uncle Jake, in all things, seemed absolutely submissive to Aunt Nancy.

But Uncle Jake was a clever old Darby at handling his Joan. He suffered from rheumatism a good deal, and Aunt Nancy made him wear red flannel drawers and undershirts all summer. Even when he was plowing in the garden in the hot sun, he had to wear them. Uncle Jake would go, most obediently, out to the garden to plow; and the very first thing he did there was to hide behind some tall bushes and take off his red flannels. He would conceal them quite carefully under the leaves of the bushes. When Aunt Nancy called him in the evening, he would put on his red flannel underclothes and go innocently home to his cabin.

Dear old Uncle Jake had the most beautifully venerable face I ever saw. We were little devils and we often hid his red flannels so that, when Aunt Nancy called him, he couldn't find them anywhere. He would go muttering around, "What dem chillun done wif my clo'es?" and poking patiently in all the bushes until we finally burst, laughing, upon him with the missing garments in our hands.

We caused Uncle Jake no end of trouble, trailing behind him and coaxing him to let us help milk the cows, or ride his horse to water while he trudged along in the dust. But he never held anything against us; and he kept each and every one of us from just punishments almost every day.

Once he threw himself between my small sister Mary, and a maddened charging cow, and he saved her literally by a gnat's nose from being tossed into the air. All of us older children had fled quickly to the fence, where we sat as safe and excited as if we had ring-side seats at a bull fight. We did not even think of the danger to which the old man had subjected himself as we rushed home to tell Mother of the thrill we had experienced in seeing Mary rescued. And we regarded Mother with surprise and curiosity when she shed tears over the beautiful faithfulness of Uncle Jake.

Perhaps one reason we did not think of Uncle Jake's danger was because he always seemed to be on such intimate terms with the animals on the farm. We considered that he knew exactly how to deal with them, for he would talk to them just as if they were people, telling them the current gossip, and unloading upon them all of the repressions of his home life.

It was nothing to us to hear Uncle Jake carry on a long conversation with a horse—punctuated by extended pauses now and then, as if he expected the horse to make answer. I always thought the horse did answer and that Uncle Jake understood its language.

Uncle Jake's conversations would go like this:

"Git up dar, Hoss, you lazy bones.—You heerd me say, git up. I's gwine beat your rump. You got a big enough one. . . .

"Well, Hoss, we's jest got one mo' row to plow.—Look at dem black clouds.—If we don't hurry up de rain comin' 'fo' we kin finish.—I tole you yistiddy de crops gwine fail if we don't git rain.—You ought to be glad to git rain as I is. Mo' hit rain now mo' we gwine eat next winter. . . .

"Nancy call us now, Hoss. We jest did git thoo in time.—Come tomorrer we got to haul wood.—Man up dar in de White House what dey calls Uncle Sam, he says folks in dis country cuttin' down too many trees.—Howsomever, folks got to have wood fo' de winter, ain't dey, Hoss?—Dat man up dar in de White House, he's a 'Publican, anyway. Folks down dis way don't think much of 'Publicans.—De Good Book say 'Publicans is same as sinners."

To a cow he would say:

"Stand over dar, Cow.—Back yo' laig, I say.—Dat's good. Nancy on de rampage agin las' night.—She say, I wars out my clo'es faster'n she kin patch 'em.—Sometimes, hit seems lak I can't please Nancy.—Women is funny people, Cow. You can't guess 'em. You got to 'sperience 'em. . . .

"Well, John Baxter beat his old 'oman agin las'

night.—I heerd her hollerin' clean up to my house. —Hit's a shame 'way he treats her, ain't it?"

Uncle Jake discussed small gossip and family affairs with the cows and sheep, but with horses and pigs he usually selected the broader field of crops, politics or religion. And he always said "Hoss" and "Cow" and "Hawg" in speaking to them. There was something universal in his attitude, for he never called them by name, but in a pen full of pigs the very pig he was talking to seemed to be perfectly aware that Uncle Jake had singled him out for confidence.

Old Mamie had an even more lasting effect upon my life than did Aunt Nancy and Uncle Jake. It was she who first told us ghost stories, and to this day I am afraid of the dark. Aunt Nancy was far too genteel and well-trained to tell children anything so bad for them as ghost stories.

But Mamie had not been raised as a house servant. She gathered and cleaned vegetables, churned, and washed clothes. Sometimes, when there was a crowd of guests, Mother had tried letting her help Jimmy Thomas wait on the table. However, this didn't work because Mamie always joined in the conversation. When anyone at the table said anything clever or startling, she would blurt out:

"Dar Gawd!" Sometimes she would say, "Well, Jesus! Don't dat take de rag off de bush!"

49

Sometimes the guests would laugh when Mamie came out with remarks like this. Sometimes they would look shocked, and sometimes they kept their faces absolutely wooden, trying to spare my mother's feelings. When they happened to laugh at what she said, Mamie would warm up to them considerably. She would give her skinny thigh a resounding smack and laugh out loud at everything they said from then on. And she made remarks more frequent and pungent.

Mamie was constantly promising my mother that she would behave in a more becoming manner. But she always became so diverted by what was being said that she never could keep her promises. After many trials and failures, Mamie was not allowed to come into the dining room any more. This was a great disappointment to her.

Mother used to say that Mamie was part Indian. She was a light, coppery brown and she had high cheekbones and a thin aquiline nose. She smoked a corncob pipe.

Mamie had two daughters who used to work for us, nursing children and doing odd jobs around the house. She had never named her two daughters, although they were grown girls; one she called "Daughter" and the other "Sis."

My father often found cause for embarrassment

in front of his guests on account of Mamie's two daughters. He would thoughtlessly call out:

"Daughter, I wish you would amuse the children around at the other side of the yard." Or he would say, "Sis, I want you to bring some clean towels up to Mr. Minor's room."

The quizzical glances Father's friends would turn on him after such requests were quite funny. And Father's position was made more comical on account of the fact that Mamie's husband, Jack, was a mulatto and her daughters were almost white.

One day in exasperation, my father said, "Damn it, Mamie, I can't keep calling those girls 'Daughter' and 'Sis.' Hang it all, you will just have to name them."

So Daughter was named "Millie," and Sis was named "Hallie." We never knew how Mamie chose their names.

Besides the colored people who lived on our place, my mother had a very special Negro friend named Becky Leftwich. Her father had belonged to the Leftwich family and, as was customary, he had taken their surname for his own. My mother herself was a member of the Leftwich clan. Therefore, on Mother's very first visit to Bedford County, Becky had come over to claim her patronage, which is also a custom with the colored people. After that, every summer when we came to Bedford, my mother brought up several bolts of longcloth which Becky Leftwich made into underclothes for us children. In other words, she did our "plain sewing." For the boys it was really plain. But for us girls the garments Becky made were so resplendent with pin tucks and Hamburg ruffles that I often wondered why Mother called it "plain sewing." At any rate, Becky Leftwich took great pride in these garments.

She took great pride in working for Mother, and she took particular pride in me, because my name was Rebecca, too. She maintained that I was her namesake, and each summer, on her first visit to us, she would bring me a baby chicken to raise. She would say that by the time we got ready to go back to town the chicken would be big enough to eat. But I never let anyone touch so much as a feather of one of my chickens.

One summer when Becky Leftwich came to our house to get her bolts of longcloth she was very sad. She sat in Mother's room and cried and cried.

"Miss Rose," she said between her sobs, "it's on account of Emma. Emma done got herself in trouble."

My mother was terribly concerned about Becky's young daughter, Emma. She tried her best to comfort Becky, but Becky only wept deeper and louder into her gingham apron.

Finally my mother said, "Becky, don't carry on like this. It doesn't help matters any. If you will only stop crying and tell me who is responsible for Emma's condition, I will talk to Mr. Yancey about it. It may be that he can make the young man marry Emma."

At that, Becky did stop crying. She raised her face out of her apron and burst into sudden peals of laughter:

"Lawd, Miss Rose, 'tain't no use to try dat. Emma, she jest like a rabbit, runnin' through de brier patch. All de briers done scratch her."

She continued to laugh with genuine amusement as she picked up the bolts of cloth and walked out of the house, leaving my pretty young mother in a great state of embarrassment, and no little disillusionment.

CHAPTER V

About Outdoor Life

wwv

THERE were so many of us that we were quite large children before my father ever got used to our names. Mother had named us. She had always selected the name of someone in either family who was distinguished or beautiful. My father was not as well up on genealogy as Mother was, and so he couldn't always remember whom she had picked. More than half the time he just called us "baby" or "son" or "little lady."

Father loved to be in the country. He taught us all to ride and shoot, and often one of us was chosen to take an all-day fishing trip with him. When I was barely nine years old I was singled out to go on one of these fishing trips with Father. We were to fish in distant Little Otter River, and Father and I set out on horseback early one morning. My fat little legs hardly reached across the horse. By the time my saddlebag was filled with lunch, fishing tackle and bait, and a large basket for fish was attached to the saddle, there was decidedly more of equipment than there was of me.

All day we fished up and down Little Otter. We had a gorgeous time. The whole sky was flying sunset banners before Father realized we should have started home long ago. Then he tried to take a short cut through the mountains and completely lost his bearings.

Wild pictures of having to spend the night in the lonely hills crowded into my mind. Old Mamie had often told me hair-raising stories of how bears and wolves devoured hunters who were lost in the woods. They tore them limb from limb while their agonized shrieks rose to high heaven. But only the owls heard, and they would say "who—who," which meant that by morning you couldn't tell who the hunters had been.

I had believed Mamie's tales implicitly, and I fully expected to fight for my life all night. However, I did not want my father to know I was afraid, so I said nothing, but sat very tight and tense on my horse as we wandered in and out of the narrow mountain trails.

Father did not guess what was going on in my childish imagination. He was not at all perturbed by our predicament.

55

"Well, baby, we are lost," he said cheerfully. "We'll see where we come out."

Sure enough we soon did "come out"—in front of a little shack in a clearing.

My father rode up to the place with the air of a knight in armor. The mountain family was having supper around the kitchen table and a tall, lean "ole woman," holding a long-handled frying pan full of bacon, came to the door.

"Madam," said my father, as if he were addressing the Queen of Sheba at the very least, "Madam, my little daughter and I have lost our way, and I'll be very grateful if you will direct me to the Forest Depot road."

His tone implied that he was a very special person for whom it would be an honor for a lady of her standing to do a favor. The woman was impressed. She invited us in to meet the family and to have supper. Two barefoot boys were sent out to feed our horses—another was dispatched to the springhouse for cool buttermilk.

Making himself perfectly at home, my father put away an amazing amount of supper.

"I tell you, sir," he said to the "ole man" who sat in overalls smoking his clay pipe after the meal, "there is no food in this world that can touch good, fresh buttermilk, and corn bread cooked in the ashes."

The "ole man" agreed with a pleased nod and a twinkle of his eye between puffs on his pipe.

My teeth felt somewhat gritty—but Father was having a lovely time. He exchanged crop news and weather news with our host, and then they swapped some tales which must have been quite fundamental, for they both laughed a good deal. While this was going on, the "ole woman" made each of her four boys and her small daughter take turns at swinging me in a grapevine swing.

When good manners permitted us to go our way, my father shook hands with each member of the family, and he made me give my blue handkerchief to the small daughter, saying to our hostess:

"Madam, I am sure my little daughter would like to give your little girl a present. Baby, what have you got with you that this child would like?"

Naturally, on a fishing trip, I had very little that was detachable. I could think of nothing but my blue handkerchief. I loved my blue handkerchief. Grandmother had given it to me with a blue hair ribbon for my birthday. Grandmother had hemstitched the handkerchief herself. She had sewed beautiful lace on it. I did not wish to give up my blue handkerchief. But there it was, sticking out of my pocket. Father's eye had already settled on it, and a certain light in Father's eye forbade any hesitation on my part.

57

My father found a number of things in his pockets for the four boys. There were pocketknives of several sizes, some fishing tackle, and an Ingersoll watch which he always carried on hunting and fishing trips, for fear of losing his father's gold one. He also had sundry other small articles that boys like, and all of these things he divided out with an impartial hand. He found for our host a can of Prince Albert smoking tobacco; but when he came to the good wife he had nothing to offer.

"Madam," he said, with as much ceremony as if he had just given each member of the family a pearl of price, "your hospitality makes me ashamed that I am not a woman. In that case, I would have about me some appropriate present for you. As it is, I can only thank you for your kindness."

The woman seemed just as well satisfied with this flowery speech. She piled courtesy upon hospitality and sent the two largest boys, mounted upon one mule, to show us the main road. With such assistance we soon were well on our way home.

The very next day, Father sent Uncle Jake miles into the mountain to take the "ole woman" a large basket of fruit and a box of "foolishness" which he had asked Mother to get together for her. He instructed Uncle Jake to invite the whole family down to spend the day with us. And when they came, my father made us all put every bit as much effort in

58

entertaining the mountain children as they had in amusing me.

Aside from riding, fishing and shooting, my father's dearest hobby was the swimming pond, which he claimed he had built for us.

Father had wanted to be an engineer. He got the stimulus for this ambition at the Virginia Military Institute under the tutelage of "Mike" Brooke, who invented the Brooke gun and who revolutionized naval warfare when he refitted the *Merrimac*. John Mercer Brooke was one of Father's idols and, from the time he first set foot at V. M. I., he wanted to grow up to be like him.

But Grandpa had persuaded Father to study law. He wanted Father in his office. I think my father believed that if Grandpa had not interfered with his career, he would have been as famous an inventor as J. M. Brooke or his friend and associate, Matthew Fontaine Maury, "Pathfinder of the Seas." And it is probably just as well that Grandpa interfered.

So Father worked off much of his thwarted engineering ambition in the building of a swimming pond "for the children." He always constructed it so that the dam would break with the spring freshets from the mountains. Then he could have the pleasure of building it all over again each summer.

My mother said Father spent enough money in cement each year to take the whole family to Europe; and my father said a healthy outdoor life was better for us than Europe. Then Mother said she was tired of nursing sunburned backs at night after we had been swimming all day.

The pond really was the cause of many trials for my mother. There were usually four or five of our little friends from Lynchburg staying with us in the summer. They came and went in different relays, and what with her own children blistering and peeling and blistering again, and new children coming in all the time and blistering and peeling and blistering again, there was always someone in the house howling with sunburn. My mother sat up all of many a night rocking the less stoical to sleep, or applying sunburn lotion to blisters.

Aside from sunburn, what the swimming pond did to our appetites was something terrific. My mother could never have enough food cooked to completely satisfy seven hungry children of her own, about four extra youngsters, and a perfectly ravenous husband besides.

Father had a dreadful appetite, and it was awfully hard upon Mother to see him enjoy such enormous quantities of food without ever gaining an ounce in weight. There was no justice in it. Sometimes at the table she would watch him with a really pained expression on her face. Sometimes, in her mild Victorian way, and in the absurd Victorian manner of being formal with husbands, she would say,

"Why, Mr. Yancey, you ought not to eat so much. It isn't good for your heart and kidneys."

"Damn it," Father would answer, "my organs are my servants, not my masters. I eat what I please and it is their business to adapt themselves to it. I won't spend my life catering to my heart and kidneys."

Sometimes Father would get bored with the swimming pond being full all summer. In the height of the season, he would pretend that something was wrong with the dam, and he would drain out all the water. Then lots of bags of cement would come up from Lynchburg, and all the farm hands and horses would have to stop their work and haul it. This always happened when Father was taking his vacation. Every morning he would put on dreadful-looking old clothes and he would go out and round up all the colored men on the place to help reconstruct the swimming pond.

Smoking always presented great difficulty during times of construction, so my father took to chewing tobacco while he was engineering. He would sit on a hod or a big rock and, directing his laborers, he would say:

"Hey, Tom, put that batch of cement right over there. That place needs reinforcement.—Not there,

damn it; I mean right over here where I spit this
tobacco juice."

Chewing tobacco was a very useful habit to Father
in his engineering. It saved him many steps. But
Mother would never let him do it around the house.

CHAPTER VI

Pests

vvvv

WHEN my father was a boy there had been
enough servants, who of course were never called
slaves, to smooth out all the bumps of life for him.
Even after the war, a good many of them stayed
with Grandma and Grandpa. My father, therefore,
grew up to think that life owed him a smooth road
to travel. By the time Father got married, a number
of these old colored people had gone to their reward,
and he thought it was Mother's business to see that
everything went along for him like oiled machinery.

My mother would have loved to have the household machinery move as if it were well oiled, pro-
vided it did not require any great exertion on her
part. But she belonged to a school which believed
that right would prevail, regardless of human effort.
Things always untangled themselves by the hand of

God and, after all, she was not God. God sent people large families, and everyone knew that large families caused a great deal of confusion. It was not her fault that large families caused confusion. It was just a fact, and one might as well accept it with a tranquil spirit.

This philosophy simplified Mother's position, but my father was greatly annoyed at anything that inconvenienced him around the house. There were a large number of things that inconvenienced him, and these he classified as "pests."

Father was very particular about his cold bath in the morning. Before we had plumbing in our house in the country he had built himself what he called a bathhouse, next to the well. This was another one of his engineering feats. On top of the bathhouse he had constructed a large tank which each morning was pumped full of water for Father's bath.

Descending from the tank, through a hole in the roof, my father had fitted an iron pipe which overhung his tub, and on the end of this pipe was one of the funniest-looking shower gadgets that human eyes ever beheld. Father had made it himself. And Father had also assisted the plumber in the construction of his tub. It was in the shape of an ordinary bathtub, though of extra large size, and it was fashioned from galvanized iron. Every morning my father would go out to his bathhouse and stand under an icy spray of cold mountain water. And when the icy water hit the galvanized bathtub it sounded like a barrage of artillery fire; and you could hear Father spluttering and splashing and singing "La Paloma" for almost a mile. If you closed your eyes you would get the sound effects of a Mexican bombardment.

Grandma's house was equipped with old-fashioned "hat tubs" which were painted pink, blue, lavender, green or yellow, to match the bedrooms which they graced. My father thought all the family should use those "hat tubs" except at given times. If he ever went out to the bathhouse and found the door locked because one of us was standing under his icy-cold shower when he wanted to be there, he would shout at the offender that he was a "pest." It was all right for us to be there when his bath was not slated, but at that particular time we were just plain pests. If the soap and towels were ever used up before he got there, that was a pest too.

Another pest was flies. We children never thought much about them; but Father considered them dirty. He had the Old Testament idea about things being unclean. Flies disgusted him and he had screens put in the house long before most people used screens. But even then, in the country, with stables and pig pens near by, and so many children running in and

65

out of the house, there were always flies to contend
with. If a fly got on my father's bald spot, or if he
even saw one zooming around a room, he almost
had a fit.

The flies irritated Aunt Nancy almost as much as
they did Father. You could hear her scolding them
while she was setting the table: "G'wan away from
here, you devils.—You can scatter all over this house
and pester everybody to death in every bedroom—
but jest as soon as I puts a meal on de table here you
all come jest lak you had a written invitation."

We had in our dining room what must be a dis-
tinctly Southern contraption to shoo the flies off the
table. At least, I have never seen one anywhere else.
It was a large oblong fan made of layers of different-
colored paper. Each layer was scalloped, and each
color showed a little below the other. This affair
hung over the dining-room table, and there was a
long cord attached to it. During mealtimes a little
colored boy would stand over against the wall by
the china press, and he would pull the fan back and
forth by means of the cord. It kept up a pretty good
breeze, shooed the flies off the table and, in action,
it appeared to my childish eyes as beautiful as the
aurora borealis.

My father thought this contraption was fine until
one day a screw in it came loose, and the whole
thing fell on his head. It bounced from there to the

gravy bowl and splashed gravy into Father's eyes, and then Father said the thing was a damned pest. Nothing in Mother's house, he fumed, ever stayed in repair. He would never let Mother put the fan up again because he insisted that it gave him indigestion to have it wigwagging over his head. He got a lot of fly swatters, and he told us we would have to go to work.

The worst pest that Father had to put up with was what he described as an utter lack of discipline in any of Mother's children. He had gone to V. M. I. at an early age. He belonged to a military era, and when the captain spoke he expected every private to fall in line. Everybody was a private except my father. But Mother had not gone to V. M. I., and whenever one of us needed discipline she did not know how to administer it. According to her ideas, vengeance belonged to the Lord, and she was perfectly content to leave it there.

Father was extremely careful of his personal possessions. He had a pair of simply marvelous military brushes, for instance, and they were the best brushes I ever saw for straightening out the tangled mass of a doll's hair. Whenever my father started to use his brushes and found them all matted up with doll's hair, he would yell that this was a damned pest. He would call my mother and ask her what in the hell was all of this long, blond hair doing in his brushes.

My mother did not have blond hair. Her hair was brown. But she knew where the blond hair had come from, and she would get it out of Father's brushes.

"Rosebud," my father would then say, "you will just have to do something to inculcate in these children some respect for the rights of others. They are a lot of damned pests. How do you expect to raise them up to be law-abiding citizens if you do not discipline them?"

"The children are just like all other children," Mother would answer amiably. "They will outgrow their mischief. Nobody in either of our families has ever done anything very dreadful. Let the children learn from experience."

Once Father decided to beat experience at its own game. And that was the time we worked an experiment on one of his favorite apple trees.

Thomas Jefferson, with his passion for distributing horticultural samples, had given the parent of this apple tree to my great-grandfather, and its offspring had been nursed very carefully and redistributed for generations. The fruit of the tree became very beautiful in July, but did not ripen until about the end of August. And the apple tree grew beside the path which led to the spring and from there on to the swimming pond.

One hot July afternoon, when I was about nine

years old, we were going for a swim and, as we were passing the favorite apple tree, Elizabeth said:

"You know, I read in the newspaper that the fruit we get from Florida is picked a long time before it is ripe. It is shipped all over the country, and by the time it gets where it's being sent, it is ripe enough to eat."

None of the rest of us ever read anything in the newspapers except the funnies. We were impressed.

"Now look at those apples," continued Elizabeth. "We could pick all those apples and store them in the cellar, and see if what the newspaper said is true."

Every one of us was enchanted with the idea. Without considering consequences or even thinking of selecting less important apples for our experiment, we dropped our bathing suits and skinned up the tree. We pulled all the fruit we could reach, and we shook the branches until not a single apple remained upon them. Then down we came. We next tied up the lower apertures of our bathing suits with some cord which one of the boys had in his pocket and we filled each of these improvised bags with apples. There were five of us and two visiting children, so we had seven bulging bathing suits full of fruit. The bags were a funny sight. We laughed as we stuffed them full and we left very few apples on the ground.

With our heavy burdens we struggled back to the house and carefully we laid all the apples in neat rows on the cellar shelves. Elizabeth insisted that not a single apple should touch another and it took us some time to arrange them to her satisfaction.

It was quite late when finally we went for our swim; so late, in fact, that my father came back from Lynchburg while we were still in the pond.

Father's daily ceremony, when he returned from town, was to walk down to the spring to get himself a "good cool drink of fresh country water." For my father said "the human body is like a swimming pool, it has to have plenty of fresh water flowing through it all the time in order to be healthy." On his daily walk to the spring, Father would contemplate with pleasure whatever crops lay on either side of the path, and he never failed to pause and look lovingly at the beautiful fruit of his favorite apple tree.

On this particular day, when Father found the branches of his apple tree perfectly bare, and a few forlorn apples lying around on the ground, he shot back to the house as if he had been fired from a cannon, and he raised a great rumpus.

Mother did not know what had become of the apples. Maybe Aunt Nancy had picked them to cook.

My father could not conceive of Nancy doing

such a thing. She knew that that apple tree was not to be touched. Nevertheless, he went storming out to the kitchen to give her a piece of his mind.

Aunt Nancy had not taken the apples. But she had seen a lot of apples in the cellar when she went down there to get out the potatoes for dinner. She had also seen the "chillun" going into the cellar with something that looked like great big bags.

My father rushed off to the cellar. There was enough circumstantial evidence at hand for him. He tore back around the house to find Mother and he told her this was the end of his endurance; we would just have to be punished. Mother sat on the porch and serenely rocked her chair while he delivered her a sermon on the subject of her many failures in the business of raising children.

About this time the whole gang of us came around the corner of the house innocently dangling our wet bathing suits. We had unwittingly walked into the very middle of a hot skirmish and our two little visitors took instant flight in the direction of the barn, but we Yanceys stood our ground.

My father accused us of having ruined his whole summer by our inconsideration and insubordination and by our utter damned thoughtlessness. We explained our reasons, but that did not help at all. Father went out to the flower garden and he broke a long switch from a young tree.

"Now, Rosa, it is your duty to manage these children, not mine," declared my father. Grimly he handed Mother the switch.

"Why, Mr. Yancey," said my mother, "I can't possibly whip all these children. It would wear me out. Besides, I don't think they have committed such a terrible crime."

My father glared at her. "All right!" he replied and, with a give-me-the-dagger look, he snatched the switch from Mother's hand.

He ordered us all to go into his own room, which was on the first floor, just off the porch. There he made us take our places around the sides of the room with our faces to the wall.

This was the first time any of us had ever been confronted with any form of corporal punishment. For my part, I felt that the very foundations of the earth were trembling, but I quickly sensed which side of the room my father would begin whipping first, and I took my place at the other side, seeking to put off the evil moment.

By the time Father got us all submissively lined up around the room, he had worked off a great deal of his steam. Perhaps he, too, felt that the foundations of the earth were trembling; or perhaps we just looked very small and helpless and he lost his convictions. However, as Elizabeth was the first in line, he gave her bare legs a few cracks with his switch. This only made Elizabeth rebellious.

"You will never make *me* cry," she said scornfully. "I haven't done anything I think is wrong and you won't have the satisfaction of hearing me make a sound."

Such defiance thrown in his teeth whetted Father up a little for his encounter with Bob. Here was another kind of personality. At the first whack, Bob yelled as if he were about to be murdered. I almost jumped out of my skin. It must have scared my father too, because when he got to Mary and Joe, I could hear only a few light strokes of the switch and they were giggling at the amount of noise Bob continued to make.

All of this time, my mother's measured rocking on the porch was plainly audible, like the steady beat of a drum, underneath Bob's shrill obbligato.

When Father got to the end of the line where I had taken my stand his switch had lost most of its mettle, and so had he. Out of the corner of my eye, I could see an absolutely stricken look on his face as Bob kept up his yelling; and I got only a couple of half-hearted taps on my fat little calves.

Then my father had to go back to the porch and face Mother. By this time our two visitors, John Ambler Nicholas and Virginia Strother, had made bold to come to the house. They were sitting on the porch with Mother looking very prim and pious, and this gave my father the cue for a properly forceful moral to his little drama which had so nearly turned into a comedy. He regarded them with a stern and righteous eye:

"Now, Virginia and John Ambler, I know that you were as much to blame in this matter as my own children, but I cannot punish you. I invited you to spend the summer here because your fathers and mothers are my friends. If, in the future, you cannot behave yourselves like the ladies and gentlemen I know your parents to be I shall have to take you home."

This resounding speech to a thoroughly meek audience saved the day for my father and entirely restored his sense of being master of the situation. He took his seat on the porch, and proceeded to unfold his evening paper with the complete satisfaction of a man who can say in his soul, "We have met the enemy and they are ours."

CHAPTER VII

Town House

vvvv

OUR house in Lynchburg was on a section of land which my great-grandfather, Henry Davis, had bought when the town was laid out. He had given Grandma a city block as a wedding present and he had built a house on it for her. Our house was certainly a far cry from the grand, imposing and stately mansions one reads about in Southern fiction. And I believe I have seen enough of houses in this state to say that very few homes in Virginia do answer to such grandiose descriptions. The large majority of old houses in Virginia are the nice unpretentious homes of nice unpretentious people. They are surrounded by the adorably unconventional gardens of people who love flowers and trees, and who do not go in for ostentation at all. Our own home was only a sweet old house, roomy and comfortable for its time, but it was filled with memories which we loved.

During its early history, Lynchburg had been the largest dark-leaf tobacco market in the world, and so it made a comparatively quick recovery after the War Between the States. In fact, right after the war, my grandfather was not so totally poverty-stricken as were most Southern people, since he was a lawyer, and his whole income had never been dependent upon a plantation. He was poor, of course. At that time, in the South, it was a disgrace for anyone to have money. It meant only one thing. But Grandpa, on account of his profession, was not absolutely cut loose from all moorings, and I suppose that is one reason why Father always took so much for granted. In a generation which was drenched in poverty, he had enjoyed some few ante-bellum luxuries.

It was only about ten years after General Lee's surrender at near-by Appomattox when Father went to the University of Virginia. Yet, even so soon after the war, he took with him his colored man, Sam. In those days the likes of Sam were called "body servants," and, as far as I can make out from various conversations overheard, Sam's main duties were to take care of Father's clothes and horses and to steer him safely back to his rooms if he happened to get plastered.

76

After Father finished at the university, he and Mr. Randolph Harrison, Mr. Armistead Long and Mr. "Willie" Dudley set up bachelor's quarters at our house in Lynchburg. Sam was installed as major-domo and he must have had his hands full in order to arrange for the comfort and convenience of so many young gentlemen. However, from all accounts, Sam simply worshiped his young gentlemen —and they loved him. They were all budding legal talent, but Father was the only one who was interested in local politics, and he was soon Mayor of Lynchburg.

In that period of military ardor which usually follows a war, every young man of Lynchburg joined some military organization. Father, on account of his training at V. M. I., was Captain of the Home Guard, but only once was he ever called into active service. This was when the governor ordered out the state militia to suppress some coal strikes at Pocahontas. I am quite sure those coal strikes did not amount to a full-fledged war; nevertheless, to hear Father describe his military activities, you would have thought that they did. He was even more proud of his record as a soldier than he was of his engineering talents. When Governor Fitzhugh Lee appointed him an honorary Colonel on his staff, it was a thorn in Father's flesh. He was afraid his actual military career would be eclipsed by vainglory and, when one of his friends greeted him on the street as "Colonel," he was furiously resentful.

"Look here, Nat," he said, "if you are so partial to military titles, I wish you'd call me 'Captain.' I'd rather be a fighting captain any day than a damned gold-lace colonel." Starting from this, as time wore on, everybody around Lynchburg did call Father, "Captain Bob."

By the time he was married Father had a great many unreformable bachelor habits. Sam had spoiled him so much that he was absolutely helpless if he dropped a collar button, and he would yell like fury for Mother to come and find anything he lost. My mother said Father would not have married at all if Sam hadn't died.

"When I married your father," Mother would say, "I was supposed to be getting the catch of Lynchburg—and the longer I live with him the more convinced I am that there *was* a catch in it for me." Mother, in this frame of mind, could say "your father" in a tone of voice which implied that all of Father's failings were the fault of that child of his from whom she happened to be soliciting sympathy. It was very annoying. She did not stop to think that we never even saw the man until long after she had selected him to be our father.

My mother was always shocked at the way Father

swore. It was years before she realized that his swearing was purely oratorical, and had no sinister intent. When Father used the Lord's name, she would remind him of the Commandment on that subject. But Father had no sense of guilt. He said he saw no harm in calling upon God to witness all the small affairs of man. The Bible taught us that God was interested in everything that befell His children and, my father said, he called upon God in acknowledgment of that interest. He said to "take the Lord's name in vain" meant swearing to a falsehood in God's name; and that was something he would never dream of doing. Then Mother would remark, looking around at us children for approval, that none of the men in her family had ever used bad language. All of her people were sweet and even-tempered. They never roared and stormed around the house when things went wrong.

But Mother must have been a poor judge of childish reactions. Her picture of the sweet, amiable family circle from which she came never stimulated any admiration in us. Father belonged to a generation closer to the belief in the divine right of kings and other gentlemen; he was closer to pagan times, when men associated on terms of comparative equality with gods. We all knew that such language as Father used was not for us. At the same time, we rather gloried in his prerogative. When Mother said her family did not indulge in such expletives, it made them seem somewhat underprivileged people in the opinion of her children.

And as for Father, he could never stand the idea of so much perfection as Mother claimed for her family. He said none of the men in her family had enough originality to swear as he did. They couldn't put the right words together.

"Well," my mother said, "I put self-control above originality."

"Petrified Peter!" my father snorted. "Refraining from swearing is not the only form of self-control. Think that over."

But Mother did not pause to think that over: "Why, Mr. Yancey, the names of the Saints are sacred. It is a serious thing to use their names lightly."

"I am serious," answered Father. "If Peter wasn't changed to stone, nothing ever was."

Father was fond of alliteration as a means of self-expression, and at times, when he got excited, he would come out with the most ridiculous word combinations imaginable. As a rule, his alliterations were perfectly harmless, like "bilious Bonaparte" or "naked Neptune"; but when he got *very* excited they became more startling. My mother, however, did not like even the harmless combinations, because such things as "bilious Bonaparte" and "naked

80

Neptune" conjured up mental pictures which no lady should contemplate.

Sometimes even Father himself was surprised at the Olympian quality of his own ejaculations. Then he would often be seized with a spirit of humility, and say that such sheer beauty was not original with him; he had got it from old General Jubal A. Early.

One of Father's favorite stories about General Early was told occasionally to select male audiences, but I have overheard it many times when I wasn't supposed to be anywhere around. It always began: "Did I ever tell you about the time the house fell on old Jubal Early?"

General Early was a privileged character around Lynchburg in his old age, for he had saved the city from being captured by the Yankees; but that did not keep the city from condemning as unsafe an office building he owned on Main Street. The work of pulling down this building had already begun, but General Early had not finished getting all of the things out of his office, because the men whom he had engaged to move his furniture had been late arriving. Being partly established in new quarters, the old General remembered some important papers he had left behind. He needed these papers at once and he went back to his old office to get them. He was sitting at his desk, poking around in the pigeon-holes when the entire building collapsed.

Though there was no hope of finding the old man alive, the fire departments and all of the military organizations of the town were called out to rescue General Early; and my father, being Mayor and Captain of the Home Guard, was in charge of the operations. After hours spent in frantic work of throwing out timbers, bricks and mortar, they finally located the General. He was entirely uninjured. The room he was sitting in had merely dropped, floor and all, to a lower level and a few timbers had formed an arch of protection over him. There he sat with his old campaign hat still on his head and, white with plaster, he calmly waited to be dug out.

When the old man looked up and saw my father in charge, he called out:

"Hey, Bob! blast my hat to hell, I didn't know you were up there, boy! I can direct these fellows for you. Damn it, you go and get me a julep."

My father hastened away and he soon brought back a small split basket in which there were several glasses of julep, packed solidly around with paper. He found General Early doing an effective job of directing his rescuers. The General's eagle eyes were glaring up from his pit and, as the men laid hold of the heavy beams, he was bellowing out:

"He-eave *to!* You sons of a bloodhound!" and "He-eave *ho!* You splinters of Adam!"

The rescue party were not objecting to these fancy names. They were sweating and straining rhythmically at the timbers with each command. But the old General lost all interest in his saviors at the sight of the basket full of juleps which was now lowered to him by means of a rope. He reared back at his desk, sipping mint juleps in utter contentment, while all hands finished the work of excavation.

This story as told by my father was plentifully punctuated with entirely unique embellishments, but it would not do to repeat all of the words which General Early used. Such language could be tolerated only by those whose faith in God and man alike is quite unshakable.

General Early died before I was born, but my father and Senator Daniel used to tell so many tales about him that he always seemed vitally alive to me.

Although John Warwick Daniel was known throughout this country as the most brilliant orator of his time, the fact that he had been General Early's chief of staff was the only point of pride he seemed to have, and when he and Father were together they talked so much about General Early's exploits that even when I was a small child, I could piece together a fairly good description of the Battle of Lynchburg from bits overheard. A thumbnail sketch would go like this:

In June, 1864, General Grant wrote General Hunter that the destruction of the Central Railroad and the canal on the James River were of greatest importance to the Federal cause. He ordered General Hunter to begin this campaign at Lynchburg.

As Hunter advanced from Staunton, he spread desolation before him. He burned V. M. I. with all its contents. He plundered Washington College and carried off the statue of Washington. Houses were destroyed by fire; furniture and bedding cut to pieces; and the entire country stripped of every morsel of food.

Thus warned of Hunter's intentions, General Lee, in Petersburg, sent General Early hurrying to the defense of Lynchburg. But, as General Hunter approached, the people of Lynchburg knew well enough that only a miracle could save them from destruction; for Hunter was now at Bedford City, only twenty-five miles away, while Early had eighty miles to travel.

Every soldier in the hospitals who could stand up on his legs or mount a horse went out to join the anxious band of old men and young boys who had gathered together on the western border of the town to die protecting their homes. In command of these was General Francis T. Nichols who, with only one arm and one leg left, took charge of the post and began organizing the sick, the wounded and crippled, the old men and boys into an army of defense. With them he hoped to hold the city against General Hunter, whose army numbered twenty-five thousand fresh, well-equipped, well-fed men.

If Early would only come! General Breckenridge arrived on the night of the 16th, bringing his battle-torn little command. Imboden came in with his small remnant of cavalry, and McCausland with two little brigades of gaunt, barefoot men. They took up a position on the Salem Turnpike, trying to keep Hunter in check; but gradually they began to give way, falling back on the town.

All during the tortured night of the 17th, a yard engine with box cars attached was run up and down the Southside Railroad to make the enemy believe that reinforcements were rapidly arriving.

Then the wild thrill of Tinsley's bugle call! In through the hills of Lynchburg swung General Early at the head of all that remained of Stonewall Jackson's own men: barefooted, bronzed, lean as greyhounds, trained in privation by the hand of a great leader, they were mighty sons of battle.

Out on the firing line Lieutenant Carter Berkeley, with a few guns, was doing his best to hold the breastworks when suddenly, piercing the din of the fighting, broke the sound of Tinsley's bugle! Now rebel yells that shook the very thunder of the guns! Then through the smoke came the vision of old

85

Jubal's broad, white slouch hat with its black feather! He galloped up into the exhausted defense line; he stood up in his stirrups and, shaking his fist at the enemy, he bellowed out at them:

"No buttermilk rangers after you now, you God-damned Blue-Butts!"

Of course, the old General knew nothing of what is called modern psychology, but he knew how to handle men. When he shook his fist at his foe and called them "Blue-Butts," the little army which guarded Lynchburg received a fixed image of Yankees in retreat. And that, Senator Daniel and my father would laugh, was the way the Yankees were usually seen when General Early snapped into action.

Another friend of Father's, who seems vitally alive even now, was old Mr. "Chilly" Langhorne. He and my father claimed to be some sort of kinsmen, though goodness knows how, when or why this relationship came about. I had rather be a mushroom than try to unravel the tangled mass of Virginia cousins. At any rate, when our papers used to publish some British criticism of Mr. Langhorne's daughter, Lady Astor, as an upstart American who had presumed to enter English politics, my father would snort, and he would say that, for those who were interested in such trivial matters, Nancy Langhorne belonged to an older and better family than plenty of present-day English peers. All during my childhood I had heard about old Mr. "Chilly" Langhorne and the unaccountable things he did and said. But he lived in England with his daughter, so I had never seen him. Then later I did.

One day I had just come back from school and, having put my books in the house, I was starting out of the front door. An old man was coming up our steps. When he saw me he began speaking in a very loud voice, as if he thought I might be deaf.

"Where's Bob?" he called out with no form of salutation.

"I don't know, Sir," I answered, conscious that I was showing much better manners than he. "My father hasn't come home yet."

"Well, you go in the house and find out when he *will* be here. I came all the way from England to see my old friends before I die and I am not going away until I see Bob."

The fact that he had come "all the way from England" did not strike me as being important. People were always coming to our house to see Father and they might be from almost anywhere.

I went to find Mother and I told her there was an old man on the porch who wanted to see Father.

"Did he give his name?" asked my mother.

"No."

"What does he look like?" she questioned further.

"I don't know. Just looks like an old man."

Mother decided he must be a client. "I don't think so," I differed. "I think he is a friend. He called Father 'Bob.' "

"Good heavens!" said my mother, "the garbage man might do that."

Mother made up her mind that he was a client. She was dressing and she did not want to hurry. She told me to tell the old man to make himself at home. He could come into the library if he liked or, if he preferred, he could wait on the porch. I carried out her instructions and went my way.

Mr. Langhorne waited and waited.

Finally he got tired of waiting and he went half a block up the street to call upon old Cousin Sally Didlake. She and her sister had kept a boys' school and, at one time or another, they had taught all the small boys of Lynchburg.

Mr. Langhorne rang Cousin Sally's doorbell and when she came downstairs he greeted her with open arms, expecting a warm reception. But she was very, very old and almost blind, and she drew back, for he had sent no name up to her.

"Sally, don't you know me?" exclaimed Mr. Langhorne, still holding out his arms.

"No, young man, I never saw you before."

"Oh, Sally! surely you remember *me*."

"I tell you I don't."

"Sally, you *must* remember the dirtiest, most mischievous, incorrigible and unteachable little boy you ever had in your school."

"Why, God bless you, Chilly, of course I remember you!" and Cousin Sally now accepted the outstretched arms.

Old Mr. Langhorne was quite an artist at telling a story and he especially enjoyed a joke on himself. When he came back to our house he told my father about his conversation with Cousin Sally and when he got to the part where she had said, "No, young man, I never saw you before," he and Father thought it was terribly funny. This puzzled me because, to my youthful eyes, Mr. Langhorne seemed tottering with age.

My father had the most contagious laugh of anyone I ever saw. He had a way of throwing back his head and completely abandoning himself to his mirth. You could see every one of his perfect teeth, and each tooth seemed to have an impish expression of merriment all its own. When Father laughed everyone in a crowded room would laugh too, whether they knew what it was all about or not. It was not that his laugh was loud or boisterous, but it had a quality which seemed to shed a sudden flash of light and warmth on everything within its radius.

On the night of Mr. Langhorne's last visit to Lynchburg, the whole house was kept awake on account of his talent for story-telling and Father's talent for laughing. Between dozes, after we had gone to bed, we could hear their voices like a jug full of flies, or two bumblebees in a bottle. Then peals of laughter would come through our open windows which made us laugh too and yet made us furious because we could not get back to sleep.

CHAPTER VIII

My Mother Becomes Mrs. Jellyby

wwv

FATHER and Mother were so entirely different that it is hard to understand how they got so much happiness out of being married to each other. The congeniality of most married couples appears, to me, to be based upon reaction to children and to household problems, and right there is where my father and mother seemed poles apart.

Our house in Lynchburg was always cluttered up with children of all ages, for when the children of Mother's and Father's friends had been told to scram out of the way in their own homes, they usually came to ours. Although most of the things my father liked to do with children were of an outdoor, physical nature, he could tell the most delightful stories if we happened to catch him in the mood, and he had his own method of making stories interesting. Whenever Father told us "Red Ridinghood," he called it "The Adventures of Red Ridinghood." This sounded thrilling at once, and from there he went on to make the tale an intense emotional experience. For instance, he always named Red Ridinghood for the child to whom he was telling the story, and it was "Little Mary Red Ridinghood," or "Little Becky Red Ridinghood," so that, when the wolf was finally overcome, it amounted to a personal victory for you.

It was the same with "Goldilocks and the Three Bears." In that tale the bears are victorious, so Father called it "The Bears and Little Disobedient, Meddlesome, Nosey-Posey Goldilocks," and he would name the biggest and most articulate bear for you. If Father was telling this story to a group of children, there would sometimes be eight or ten bears—a whole pack to set upon the unfortunate Goldilocks. He would name each bear for a member of his audience and introduce extra articles of furniture and toys for all of them. There were skates and bicycles and sewing tables—anything he thought would satisfy the ambitions and longings of his small listeners; and sometimes there were baseball bats and doll carriages. Then he would give each bear some special accomplishment which was calculated to flatter the child who was its namesake. Furthermore, my father would endow those bears with great powers of penetration and deduction. Indeed, the bears that Father portrayed were the equals of Sherlock Holmes in their observations which led to the discovery of the intruder, Nosey-Posey Goldilocks. It left a child feeling proud and resourceful after the story was completed.

At those times when Father was in a humor for entertaining us, he made himself so fascinating that we hung around him to the point of suffocation. We sat all over him and on the arms of his chair, or we sprawled on the floor with our backs propped against his legs. But if we got too persistent in our demands for encores his mood would suddenly change, and he would brush us away like so many troublesome kittens:

"Scat! Scat out of my way," he would protest. And if we did not move off immediately he would just as soon step on our jack straws or kick our dolls across the floor in making his escape.

There was hardly ever a day when our house was not full of children—having a candy pull, cutting paper dolls or producing a play in practically every room. And if Father came into the house with some of his friends and found any of us in his way, he would say:

"Scat out of here, you little pests! Scat out of here! I want to use this room."

Our small friends never resented anything Father said. When he scatted them out of a room they would laugh and get going. But Mother thought he was often impolite to them.

When Mother came into the library to read and found a group of us there editing our weekly newspaper or playing charades, she would get herself a book and take it quietly away. She never "squatted upon the claim" of anyone else.

What with my father always entertaining his friends and the children always bringing in theirs, my mother gradually gave up trying to do anything about her own friends. Now and then she would buy herself an entirely new wardrobe, as a symbol of protest against the confining ruts of her life, and she would take a nice trip. But Mother really loved her own comfortable ruts. Between trips, as time wore on, she became a complete bookworm, and we began calling her "Mrs. Jellyby."

It is difficult for me to understand how anyone could become so totally absorbed in a book as Mother did. When she was reading anything that interested her, six children might be engaged in active combat under her very nose, and she would not lift her eyes nor register a single expression of annoyance. The whole house might have fallen in around her, as it did around General Early, and she would never have known it!

Once my brother Joe broke his nose playing football, and his young friend, Bob Johnson, a nephew of Senator Carter Glass, brought him home. Bob thought it best to break the news gently, so he made poor suffering Joe sit in the front hall while he went to prepare Mother for the shock. He found Mother studying some book very diligently and making marginal notes as she read.

"Mrs. Yancey," said Bob, standing very stiff and worried, "you know Joe and I have been playing football today."

"Yes—Bob—I know you have," replied my mother vaguely, never raising her eyes from what she was reading.

"Well—you know football is a pretty rough game," ventured Bob, feeling his way along.

"Yes—Bob—I understand it is." Mother did not even look up.

"Well—you know—sometimes boys get hurt playing football."

"Yes—I suppose they do—Bob," said Mother scribbling on the margin of her book.

"Mrs. Yancey," Bob blurted out in desperation, "Joe's nose is bleeding. He broke it!"

"Well—take him to the bathroom and see what you can do for him, will you, Bob?"

Bob obediently led Joe to the bathroom and together they swabbed the bloody nose. The whole place was gory and many towels were soaked red when, all at once, Mother came back to earth and realized what was going on.

She threw down her book and hurried to the bathroom to comfort Joe. Then she rushed to the telephone to call our family doctor. Next, she ran back to the bathroom and sent Bob flying over to the hospital across the street to get *any* doctor to come quickly before our doctor could get there from downtown. In a very few minutes, Joe was embarrassed with too much medical attention.

Always, after this, Mother used to say that Joe's nose was much handsomer than it had ever promised to be before it was broken. She took as much pride in the transformation as if she had broken it herself.

When we were children there were not many houses in Lynchburg that were heated with steam heat. Our house was equipped with Latrobe stoves, which were in the downstairs rooms, and which heated the rooms above by means of registers. But they were not very satisfactory for a household like ours.

Some of the younger children were always punching the isinglass out of the doors of the Latrobes, simply because they could not resist the temptation to do so. Or they would stick something into the holes of the registers upstairs, and then go running downstairs in great haste to see if it fell into the stove below. This sort of thing did not disturb Mother much, but one fall my Father reached his limit and he decided to install a furnace. When Father finally came to this decision he was working on a case which required him to go to Washington. The case could not be postponed, but neither could the furnace, for the approach of winter was imminent. However, Father did not like the idea of being absent while an interesting job of engineering was going on. The installment of a heating plant was just the kind of work he most loved to boss, and he was reluctant to leave anything so important in Mother's hands.

At this my mother rose up. Anyone would think she was a baby, she declared. Besides, Father had engaged a competent man to do the work. Mr. Mathews did not need him hanging around. She herself was perfectly capable of giving Mr. Mathews the few instructions he might want. And Mother made these comments with such unusual energy that Father was entirely taken in. He actually believed that by the time he returned from Washington the furnace would be nicely installed, and all of the confusion over and done with; and Father departed with this expectation.

Quite a few days were necessary for the workmen to prepare the cellar, which was not quite deep enough to accommodate a furnace. Next, they had to lay the cement floor and put the furnace itself in place. Mother was interested enough for these first few days, but then she got tired of the whole procedure.

By the time the men were ready to put in the pipes and to set up the radiators, Mother had begun on a very interesting book and she did not want to be disturbed. So when Mr. Mathews asked her to go around the house and show him where he was to bore holes for the pipes, and where he was to mark off space for the radiators, my mother side-stepped the issue:

"You just put them anywhere you think best, Mr. Mathews. I am sure you know more about that sort of thing than I do—anything you do will be all right."

With this assurance Mr. Mathews got busy and bored all the holes he needed in the floors, both up-stairs and down. He finished boring on a Saturday and at noon the workmen left to take their week-end of rest and diversion.

On Sunday Mother finished her book. While she was looking around in the library for something else to read, she began to notice the holes that Mr. Mathews had bored in the floors. Every hole was in the wrong place. So on Monday morning my mother met Mr. Mathews as he came in the back door and, smiling very sweetly, she directed him into the library:

"Now, Mr. Mathews, I hate to be so much trouble. But you see these old bookcases—how large they are. If we put radiators here, where you have made these holes, there will not be enough space for the bookcases."

Mr. Mathews took some chalk out of his pocket and made new marks on the floor. Then Mother got up enough momentum to show him where she wanted the radiators placed in the sitting room, the hall, the dining room—she went over the whole lower part of the house. So Mr. Mathews started his men making a new set of holes. After that, they began to get the pipes and radiators ready, and Mother went off to another book.

My mother's room was on the first floor of our house in Lynchburg. There were many days when she did not go upstairs at all, but that evening she came to a stopping place in her book and it occurred to her to go upstairs and look around at the radiator holes. Then she saw that, while the holes were all right downstairs, they had come out wrong upstairs. The radiators cut up the large wall spaces where the beds and chests of drawers had to go.

And the next morning when Mr. Mathews came back my mother met him at the door again.

"Mr. Mathews," she said in her soft voice, "I wish

you would come upstairs, if it isn't too much trouble.

"Now, you see we *can't* have that radiator there, for instance. That old bed has been right there ever since this house was built. There is no other place in this room for it, and Mr. Yancey would never consent to it being put anywhere else. Couldn't you move the radiator?

"—And come in this room, Mr. Mathews. You can see there is no other wall space for that chest of drawers, so we can't possibly have this radiator here."

Mother went from room to room, sweetly explaining her difficulties, and Mr. Mathews followed her patiently, marking more new places for pipes and radiators.

This kind of thing went on the whole day; whenever Mother got the furniture placed right upstairs the holes for the pipes were all wrong downstairs. But Mother spoke in such a pleasant voice, and she looked so pretty, that Mr. Mathews never raised any objection to the number of times she changed her mind. All that day he went about boring holes and making chalk marks for radiators wherever Mother told him, until she was satisfied.

Late that afternoon my father got back from Washington. When he walked into the hall and saw such a large number of perforations in the floor, and in the ceiling above, he fairly exploded:

"What in the hell has been going on here!"

From the hall he went into the library, which was likewise dotted here and there with neat round holes.

"Good God A'mighty! This house looks like a pepperbox!" said my father.

He had to get a carpenter and a plasterer and a paper hanger to repair all the damage Mother had done.

Bedlam

wwv

OUR house was sometimes a perfect bedlam.
Anything impossible could happen there, and anything did happen right along. My father was so ir-
repressibly himself that he had no fear at all of seem-
ing ridiculous. He was no shrinking violet and, when
he pulled off a scene, he did not care who looked
or listened.

Father was of Huguenot descent on several counts
and, whenever Mother took him to task for his utter
lack of restraint, he drew heavily upon his French
ancestry. He told my mother she was just too
damned self-consciously English for any use. He
said he admired the English people for their high
ideals of public service, but that he'd be damned if
he would let that interfere with his private life. My
mother said he had no private life. His ridiculous

behavior was public property. "Everybody in this town," she said, "is always laughing at your antics."

"Well," my father would come back, "I don't mind people laughing at me. That's one way of being popular. People like you if they can laugh at you. It makes them feel superior."

As a matter of fact, Father felt so absolutely superior himself that he did not care who felt superior to him. My mother would tell him he was *quite* English in his sense of superiority.

Our neighborhood changed somewhat as the urge for building modern houses grew. Several of the older families that had always lived near us moved to new residential sections, and a branch of the city fire department set up a station across from our house.

When we were children, those firemen across the street felt a most unwarrantable responsibility for all our goings and comings. Except in case of emergency, they had nothing much to do but sit on a line of chairs, leaning comfortably back against an iron fence in the shade of a large tree. They numbered themselves among my father's most ardent supporters for his office of Commonwealth's Attorney, and they thought that gave them part interest in all of his offspring. They were just as dictatorial as Aunt Nancy, and if they ever saw us do anything we shouldn't be doing, they would yell at us:

"Stop squirting those water pistols at everybody that passes your house. I'll tell your father if you don't." Or, "Stop that playing 'stealing rocks' in the middle of the road—next thing you know, one of you will get run over."

My father had a very fine hunting dog—a pointer, named "Kirk." Mr. Sydnor Kirkpatrick had given him to Father; so the dog had been named for him. Kirk was a wonderful companion for children and often we would bring him into the front yard to play with us. But Kirk had one awfully bad habit. Somewhere in the back of his mind, he seemed to have a reason for cherishing a violent antipathy against ladies in long taffeta petticoats that went "swish-swish." In the early nineteen-hundreds almost every lady swished.

Whenever Kirk was in the front yard and heard a swishing on the street, he would rush wildly out at the swisher with perfectly terrifying barks and snarls. Sometimes he tore ladies' skirts and once or twice he even bit. This caused no end of trouble for the firemen. They disapproved of our bringing Kirk around to the front and, when we did, they would roar at us to take that dog back where he belonged. If we refused to obey their command, they felt it their bounden duty to keep a sharp lookout on behalf of ladies in skirts. For every lady that rounded our corner, they would call out apprehensively:

"Hold that dog! Hold that dog before he kills somebody!"

Their intense excitement usually made Kirk all the more belligerent, and sometimes it took three or four of us to hold him. We couldn't always do it, even at that.

Every Saturday Uncle Jake used to drive a wagon and two large white horses down to Lynchburg. He brought us fresh eggs and butter, vegetables, logs of wood for the open fireplaces, and our clean clothes which were laundered in the country. Father thought there was nothing like milk and vegetables straight from the country; and he was absolutely convinced that it was much healthier for the clothes to be washed up there, where the air was fresh and sweet, and where there was plenty of sunshine for drying. So Uncle Jake came down each week with a wagon load of stuff. When he went back he carried the soiled clothes and what money was necessary for expenses at the farm.

One Saturday Uncle Jake had driven his team of white horses into our back yard and he was in the kitchen, waiting for his dinner, while his horses ate theirs. My brother Henry was about twelve years old, and he had selected this day to see what it would be like to smoke a cigarette. Henry's room was at the back of the house; thus it was quite private, and he had closed the door and lit up with a rather secure feeling. But, while his experiment was going on, Henry heard someone come into the next room. Hastily knocking the fire off the end of the cigarette, he put it into his coat pocket for future reference, and he hung his coat on a chair. Then he went nonchalantly downstairs.

But the cigarette was not entirely put out. My sister Mary happened to be in the back yard and in a little while she saw smoke pouring out of Henry's window. Mary came running up the back steps, broadcasting as she ran that the house was on fire.

The rest of us children were thrilled beyond words. We started racing upstairs to see the fire. But such rash action terrified Mary. She flung herself into the library, where Father was just preparing to count out the money for Uncle Jake.

"The house is on fire!" screamed Mary hysterically. "They have all gone upstairs—make them come down—*please* make them come down! The whole back of the house is burning! I saw the smoke." Here Mary burst into tears.

Father was thoroughly alarmed. He rushed to the front porch and, wildly waving his hands in the air, he scattered money in all directions:

"Fire!—Fire!—Fire, by God!" shouted Father as loudly as he possibly could shout.

My mother, in the library, looked up from her book with a bewildered expression on her face:

"Just listen to your father making a fool of himself again," she said.

I was the last child to start upstairs. When Mother made this remark and I looked out and saw three sturdy firemen come charging across the street, each armed with a fire-extinguisher, I could get no farther for a while. I sat down on the steps and laughed until tears ran down my cheeks.

In the meantime, Henry had at once sensed the cause of the fire. While four brothers and sisters stood excitedly peering into his smoke-filled room, Henry walked coolly past them, picked up the flaming coat and chair and threw both out of the window.

When the firemen arrived on the scene followed by my father, who was swearing loudly and urging them to hurry, they found much smoke but no fire.

"Where is the fire?" they asked with one voice.

"I threw it out of the window," answered Henry with a beautifully restrained smile. He was confident that his heroism would outweigh his misdemeanor.

All at once, we were conscious of a great commotion in the back yard. My father poked his head out of the window:

"Good God A'mighty!" he exclaimed, "the horses are on fire!"

We were at the windows in a jiffy. Henry's coat and the chair had landed on the backs of Uncle Jake's horses, and they were protesting mightily.

Their tails were blazing furiously and, rearing and plunging in their harness, they were about to wreck the wagon. The firemen quickly grasped the situation and, brushing aside several children, they sprayed the agitated horses from above. And that was the end of the fire, except for the burnt rumps and perfectly hairless tails of two white horses.

The greatest to-do we ever had at our house centered around a time when those two white horses did not arrive on Saturday. The weather had been very cold and Uncle Jake's rheumatism was so bad that he could not drive the twelve miles to Lynchburg.

So Julia Smith, who did our washing, sent the clean clothes by express. She sent them C. O. D.

Our house was usually bursting with people. However, as fate would have it, when the clothes came C. O. D. nobody was at home but the cook, and it also happened that the cook was new at our house. She did not have any money to pay the express charge and so the driver refused to leave the large package.

On Monday morning, when my father was ready to take his cold bath, he could not find any clean shirts or underclothes, and he got into a great temper. He stormed downstairs to Mother's room and asked her why in the hell Julia Smith hadn't sent his clothes.

Mother, very gently trying to calm him, said that

Julia had sent the clothes, but that nobody was at home to pay the charge and the young man would not leave them. After all, it was not absolutely necessary for anyone to have clean clothes *every* day. She would send one of the children down with the money right after breakfast.

"Damn it," said my father, "I want my clean clothes now. I won't eat breakfast until I have them. I can't wait around all day on the convenience of a lot of incompetent women and children. I have to be at the courthouse at ten!"

All the time Father was delivering this ultimatum, he was jerking on his bathrobe and then, with the cord trailing behind him, he stamped his way to the telephone.

"Get me that damned express office," he ordered the cook who, awe-stricken at his ferocity, stood rooted in her tracks in the act of setting the table.

"Hello—damn it, is this Mr. Blank?

"No, I don't want to speak to you. I don't want any subordinates. Damn it, I want to speak to Mr. Blank himself. . . .

"Hello, Mr. Blank—this is Bob Yancey. That young fool you sent up here Saturday refused to leave my clean clothes because nobody was here to pay him. . . .

"I don't give a damn if they are his orders. I've

got to have my clean clothes. Damn it all, do you want me to have vermin?"

Mother had followed my father to the telephone, trying to pour oil upon the troubled waters and, at this point, she was so scandalized that she took the telephone out of his hand. This is what she heard repeated patiently, and with great politeness:

"As I was trying to tell you, Cap'n Bob, the driver is just a green young country boy, blindly carrying out his orders. He didn't know who you were. I am sorry his stupidity should have caused you so much inconvenience. If he had been anything but ignorant he would have left your package."

"Mr. Blank," answered my mother in Father's stead, "I hope you will not reproach the young man. He was entirely within his rights. I am very sorry Mr. Yancey has behaved so badly."

Here Father decided that things were not going to suit him. He grabbed the receiver away from my mother.

"Damn it," he absolutely bellowed into the telephone, "I can't take my bath and dress until I have my clean clothes. And damn it, I *will* have them. You send that haggis-headed young idiot up here right now. The express company ought not to have jackasses on their pay roll!" and Father banged up the receiver.

In no more than ten minutes the package was at our door, accompanied by many apologies. My father had his bath, dressed, ate his breakfast and went serenely down town. He had immediately forgotten the whole incident.

However, my mother hadn't forgotten it. After he had left, she called the express office to thank Mr. Blank and to apologize again for Father's behavior.

But Mr. Blank would not listen to her regrets. He burst out laughing and repeated my father's tirade over and over; and he particularly enjoyed the part about the vermin, much to Mother's confusion. When Mother thought it was time to finish the conversation he kept on.

" 'Haggis-headed,' " he chuckled. "I'll have to remember that one. It's perfect—old Cap'n Bob is a catbird!"

After a long time Mother managed to say goodbye to Mr. Blank and she went into the kitchen to conciliate her new cook. Again she was sorry Mr. Yancey had lost his temper. He really didn't mean any harm at all—

"Lawd, Miss Rose, I don't mind," was the answer Mother received. "I likes to work for quality folks . . . I knowed Mr. Yancey was a 'ristocrat de minute I heerd him cuss so pretty."

Mother was always annoyed when people showed

that sort of attitude toward Father. How could she hope that he would ever conduct himself like anything but a spoiled child, she complained, when the whole town, even the colored people, conspired together to make excuses for his glaring faults.

CHAPTER X

On Procrastination

wwww

THINKING of it now from an adult point of view, and in this age of small families, I realize that Mother never could have found time to satisfy the thousands of demands of seven children, and of a very demanding husband. Mother was no organizer. But even if she had been an organizer and had adopted for herself a twenty-four-hour workday as well, she couldn't have done it.

Mother would go along sewing, mending, and directing the household quite industriously for a few days. Then she would get bored with it and she would slide into a moratorium. When Mother was having a moratorium nobody could get her to do a thing. She didn't even hear you when you asked her. It was during moratoria that we always called her Mrs. Jellyby. She would read from morning until

night, and nothing we did could distract her attention. She was simply in another world. Then she began to write poetry. She sent her poetry to magazines
and most of it was returned, but she kept on writing
it.

The only chance we had to talk to Mother at all,
during a moratorium, was at mealtimes. Then the
whole family would launch at her simultaneously—
especially her four daughters. We had begun to go
to parties and we needed this and that done at once.
Our meals were often very torrid affairs:

"Mother, why haven't you mended the lace on my
blue evening dress? You know I've got to wear it
tonight." Before Mother could answer:

"You are just mistaken if you think Mother is
going to *touch* anything of yours until she fixes that
ugly old hand-me-down coat of yours I've got to
wear this year. I don't want the coat. I don't like it.
But if I've got to wear it, I need it *now*. I asked
Mother to shorten it weeks ago—before this party
was ever heard of."

"Well, I am older than you are. I come first."

"If you think you are so grown-up, you should
know how to mend your own evening dress. You
tore it."

Sometimes if arguments got too hot my father
would leave the table. He said he couldn't digest his
food if he had to eat it in the middle of a damned

debating society. When this happened, Father would have his meal served to him later on, in solitary state, with all sorts of extra dishes added to make up for his inconvenience.

Mother, however, could maintain perfect calm through any kind of altercation. If ever there was a pause long enough for her to make a remark, she would say it was a great pity that all her children were so much like the Yanceys. She was brought up in a household where it was not considered civilized for human beings to fuss and quarrel. She was not a machine for turning out work. She would get around to all these things when she could.

But never, by any means, did Mother "get around to all these things." Bland Tucker, the son of the old Bishop Tucker, took me to my first evening party, and I shall never forget how furious I was when he had to wait for me to be sewed into my dress. For a long time I had been reminding Mother of the day, of the hour and of the very minute when I had to have that dress. She had promised to have it altered and ready, and she really meant to keep her promise; but a moratorium slipped up on her, and she didn't. When the last minute came, the dress did not have a hook on it. I had to have it sewed up on me, and this was going on downstairs in Mother's room when Bland rang the doorbell.

Mother was far from being disturbed by Bland's

arrival. She went out to speak to him and she invited him to come into the sitting room, so that she could talk to him through the door while I was being sewed up. After all these years, I can still see that door-framed picture etched by irritation: Bland Tucker sitting on the top of a quaint old desk that Senator Daniel had given my father. He was swinging his long legs and chatting away with Mother, who jerked me first to one side and then to the other as her needle traveled. They seemed to be having a grand time. Nobody was impatient but me, and I could have wrung both their necks.

After many unpleasant experiences of this kind, I gave up depending upon Mother. I learned to sew for myself and I really did quite well at it. However, Mother would not allow me to congratulate myself upon my new accomplishment. When I displayed some of my handiwork for her admiration she merely commented:

"Yes—that does rather well. You really ought to be very grateful that I am so incompetent. You know, it is only the no-account Mothers who ever raise efficient daughters." She said this with such a sweet guileless look that I did feel sincerely grateful!

My father did not fare so well as I did. During a moratorium he would have to search through all his clothes to find a shirt with the proper number of buttons, and he was the last person who would ever have thought of sewing them on for himself, since he had been accustomed to having someone wait on him all of his life.

There was one morning when Father could not find a single shirt with a complete set of buttons. He stood at his bureau and pulled every shirt out of the drawers. As he examined each one for buttons he flung it over on his bed, and for each shirt that hit the bed my father said, *"Damn* my luck!"

Finally Father grabbed up one shirt and sailed down the steps, determined to confront Mother with the evidence of her procrastination, and to get some buttons sewed on at once. But Mother was not to be found. Clad only in bathrobe and pyjamas, Father went from room to room. When he did not find Mother present he said, "Damn!" and he slammed the door with a loud bang. By the time he got to the dining room he was in an awful temper. Henry was there having an early breakfast and, finding a substitute, Father had to unload on someone. Wrathfully, he held up his shirt for Henry's inspection:

"Damn it all, son, I want to give you some advice: When you grow up, don't marry one of these pestiferous poets. You will have to go around dressed like John the Baptist."

My mother had heard Father fuming around in his room and, as he came down the back steps, she had slipped up the front way. She picked up a shirt from his bed and quickly she sewed on all the missing buttons; then she quietly went back to her own room. This was easily done, for she could spot where Father was by the uproar he was making.

Having delivered his authoritative admonition to Henry, my father again made his way to Mother's room, announcing as he went that he would have to find himself some damned safety pins and see what he could do with *them*.

There at her mirror stood Mother, innocently tucking up her long brown hair.

"Why, Mr. Yancey," she said sweetly, "you ought to be ashamed to make so much noise about nothing. I have already laid out your clean shirt and underclothes in the bathroom."

This unprecedented attention completely drew the teeth of Father's rage. With a good-humored laugh he kissed my mother on both rosy cheeks and, having come into her room like a lion, he went out like a perfect lamb, leaving Mother exceedingly well pleased with herself.

Sewing was not the only thing Mother postponed. She was the world's champion postponer. She had a real talent for it.

Our house in Lynchburg had an English basement, part of which had once been used as a dining room and a kitchen. Besides these two rooms, there were several large square storerooms with flagstone

floors that stretched away under the entire house.
This basement was ideal for Mother's procrastina-
tions. Down there were stacked hundreds of magazines, most of which held no more than one poem
that Mother wanted to save. She had had the magazines put in the basement until she "got around to"
clipping out the poems for pasting them into scrap-
books. Then there were all of Grandpa Yancey's law
books. Some day, Mother was going to sort them
over to see if anything valuable was among them,
and the rest she was going to give to anyone who
would haul them away. But the things that took up
most of the room in our basement were Mother's
"antiques."

Long before it was considered stylish to have old
furniture, Mother would have nothing else in her
house. She carefully hoarded everything old that
she could beg, either from her own family or from
Father's, all through the golden-oak and bird's-eye-
maple age. Sometimes she poked around in second-
hand stores. Sometimes she went to auction sales.
And always she was adding to the collection of old
furniture and odds and ends which cluttered up the
basement. My father used to say he was the first
"antique" Mother had become interested in, and
that was what had started her off. However this may
have been, Mother had two large basement rooms
heaped full of things: chairs piled on top of sofas;

corner cupboards laid out on tables; and footstools, mirrors, picture frames and quaint old vases, stuck in wherever they would go.

My father occasionally would complain that this mess was worse than Grandma's room in the country had ever thought of being. It was a disgrace. He said if ever those weak legs on those old sofas and tables gave way under all that junk piled on them, it was going to cause an earthquake.

My mother said it was not "junk." It was an enviable collection of rare and beautiful furniture. She was going to have every bit of it done over when she "got time to go into how much it would cost."

However, hardly anything in that basement emerged "done over." The colored people have an apt expression which exactly describes Mother's attitude with regard to her collection. Whenever they are reprimanded for having left undone something they should have done, they will say, "Yes, suh, I's sorry. I been layin' off to do dat for a long time." Just so, my mother continued "layin' off" to get her furniture done over. Of course the things were not needed in the house, and there was no reason for Father to bother about them. He never thought of them except when something unusual happened to take him to the basement—but when anything did take him there, he had much to say about the coming cataclysm.

My father could not bear the sight of a cat. It irritated him more than anything just to have one around. But once a neighbor of ours went out of town and she asked Mother to take care of her cat while she was away. This cat took a great fancy to Father, which nearly drove him wild, for, as Father sat reading his paper, she would hunch up her back in the strange manner of cats, and she would rub herself against his legs. Sometimes when she did this her tail got up inside of Father's trousers. And every time that happened Father almost had a fit.

One day, after many complaints, Father impatiently asked my mother, "When in the hell is that woman coming back to get this damned pest?" and he gave the cat a push with his foot.

My mother registered her mild protest:

"Don't push that cat around, Mr. Yancey. You know she is going to have kittens."

"Well, damn it," said my father, "I don't want her to have them in my breeches leg."

Mother, seeing that he was more annoyed with the cat than usual, picked her up with careful hands and said she would carry her down to the basement.

For a while perfect peace and quiet prevailed. Father concentrated on the afternoon paper with complete detachment. Then all of a sudden, a terrific crash broke the silence. The cat had evidently climbed up on one of Mother's weak-legged sofas, seeking a soft bed, and—the much-talked-of earth-quake had come! But like most predictions, the earthquake took its prophet unawares. My father sprang from his seat; he threw down his paper "plump" on the floor and stared wildly around. Then he understood.

"By God!" he said, "the cat's had a buffalo!"

CHAPTER XI

On Religion and Prohibition

⁄⁄⁄⁄⁄⁄

FATHER had his own views on religion, and they were quite practical as far as he was concerned. We were Episcopalians. Grandma had given the lot on which our rectory had been built. She had been one of the founders of Grace Church and Father felt that all of his family should be its loyal supporters. The rectory garden ran the entire length of the block back of our house, and when Father used to see our beloved rector, Mr. Lloyd, pottering around out there, he liked to go to the back yard and exchange advice on the proper seasons for planting various things. Mr. Lloyd was of the old school. He was both a visionary and a realist, and he and Father had a very deep understanding.

After Mr. Lloyd's time, Grace Church thought it advisable to sell the large lot of the rectory for enough profit to pay off the inevitable church debt, and a new rectory was built on a small lot nearer the church. To Father this was unthinkable. Grandma had given a third of a block for a rectory and for nothing else. It was supposed to be used as such. Who ever heard of a rectory with no garden! It was part of a ministry to associate with growing things.

Father let us understand that *we* belonged to Grace Church but, for his own part, he divided his loyalty. Although he went regularly every Sunday morning to our church, and sat quite immaculate in wing collar and striped trousers, I knew that Father did not like the sermons our new minister preached. He said he was too realistic in his spiritual-isms and too spiritualistic in his realisms. Whatever that may mean. When I questioned my father about it he said the man had got his values mixed up.

I sang in the choir and, in church, I was always conscious of Father. I thought he looked ever so dis-tinguished with his large high-bridged nose, his prominent decisive chin and his close-clipped grey mustache. But, at that, his presence was very disturb-ing to me. His electric blue eyes shot out dragons of light visible even up to the choir stalls as he agreed or disagreed with whatever theory was being pro-mulgated from the pulpit. More often than not he disagreed, and any Sunday I expected him to stand up in his pew and turn the sermon into a debate. It was always a relief when church was over with no such mishap.

I did not have to worry about Father's reactions on Sunday night. Having lost Mr. Lloyd, he found his ideal again in Dr. Paxton. But Dr. Paxton was the Presbyterian minister; and so it was that Father divided his loyalty. He went to the Presbyterian Church on Sunday night.

Dr. Paxton was Scotch and tall and spare. He was a scholarly man and a person of great dignity. He also had his own sense of humor, and he was an expert shot. Dr. Paxton's dignity and erudition, along with his typical Scotch sense of humor, would have enlisted Father's admiration at once, no doubt. But when he found Dr. Paxton a first-rate sportsman as well, that clinched the deal. It was the beginning of an enduring friendship.

And so, an odd situation came about. Our family has always been predominantly Episcopalian for the past three hundred years. But after Dr. Paxton came to Lynchburg we never had a wedding or a funeral that he was not asked to share the services with our Episcopal clergyman. None of us would have been considered legally married or buried with proper solemnity without his presence.

It never would have occurred to Father to make any special excuses for his Presbyterian affiliations, but now and then his disregard for doctrines would come out. When any of us children would ask him to explain some religious dogma, he would say there were too many doctrines in the world and too little religion. Preachers were the custodians of doctrine, but Jesus belonged to the people. Jesus was simple enough for any child to understand, and we didn't need to know doctrines. Jesus was an outdoor man. He fished and walked in the mountains. He lived close to nature and drew his lessons about God from that source. Then Father would add that he had never felt drawn to these "hothouse preachers." They were too often superficial and artificial.

Although Father went regularly to the Episcopal Church on Sunday morning, and regularly to the Presbyterian Church on Sunday evening, I have often wondered if the two guardians of his soul would not have felt that they had done a poor job on him had they known of his activities between sermons.

After morning service was over, my father would come home and change to an old pair of trousers and a shirt that might be full of holes. Then he spent the day doing carpenter work. He put up shelves where nobody had ever thought of wanting shelves. He made wooden saltboxes for the kitchen and nailed them up in the most inaccessible places possible. And he nailed them up so securely that not even Samson could have pulled them down. He invented towel racks with contraptions to prevent towels from sliding off, and medicine chests with gadgets to keep bottles from falling out when the doors were jerked open. He hacked and hammered all day.

My mother hated to have all this hammering going on during Sundays. She was always reminding Father of what the neighbors would think. My father said he didn't give a damn what they thought. He would never consider dictating to them how they should use their time. Sunday was a day of recreation and this was his recreation. He had been sitting in church all morning listening to the Reverend Doctor Blake hammer out his sermon. He didn't see any difference between hammering out a sermon and hammering in a nail. He spent his entire life trying to help people untangle their troubles and their moral problems. He'd be damned if he wouldn't have one day a week to do something he wanted to do.

For all of Father's denominational impartiality, he was in a tight spot when Prohibition became a point of loyalty in the Methodist and Baptist churches. He had always maintained that one church was as good as another—that they all ought to be one. But Father was violently against Prohibition. And when this movement got to be a church issue he was forced into a position of armed neutrality. He said one had to remember that a church was greater than the passing mistakes which some of its leaders might make.

In the days when Virginia was almost solidly behind Prohibition, Lynchburg was a veritable stronghold for the drys. The masses of the people were for it, and yet the vote in Lynchburg offered a peculiar paradox. Carter Glass fought for Prohibition tooth and nail, and he was elected over every wet candidate who ever opposed him. During that same time, Father fought against Prohibition tooth and nail, and he was elected over every dry candidate who ever opposed him.

Father was not at all shy about being seen in the camp of the enemy. He went regularly to Prohibition meetings, and, sitting in the midst of the most enthusiastic advocates of the cause, he would tease and bait them along about their views on the subject. He seemed to enjoy the fights. He loved to argue that Prohibition would not reform a single drunkard, it would only be calling the righteous to repentance.

"Now tell me, Fred," he said one night as he walked out of one of these mass meetings with a friend, "tell me—after you fellows have called all the righteous to repentance, who is going to call the sinners that all of this righteousness will make?"

"Bob, you are just trying to be perverse. Prohibition is coming. The people want it. We live in a democracy, and you are an elected representative of the people. You should support the measures they favor."

"I am not elected to represent the people," laughed Father. "I represent the law. I see the whole question from the viewpoint of legal history. You are right in saying that Prohibition will come. But it will be a failure."

"Not if it is properly enforced."

"It can't be enforced. It will promote corruption in high places. It will offer temptations that the police can't resist. It will bring about trade wars in the underworld of large cities. It will cause a wave of lawlessness all over this country which will make us the laughing stock of the whole world."

"Bob, that is fantastic. A crime wave in our well-organized country! Pooh!"

"You will see. It will take years to clean it up, and it will cost millions of dollars—to say nothing of the loss in revenue which ought to go into the Treasury."

"Bob, I never knew you were a pessimist."

"Well, I am an optimistic pessimist, for I believe that Repeal will follow Prohibition."

I confess that I, like my father's friend, thought Father was fantastic in his predictions. He used to talk so much about what was coming in the wake of Prohibition—and since so few people agreed with him, I felt that he must be wrong. Now, seeing how surely everything he foretold did come to pass, I often look back in amazement. It must be that Father had good judgment after all. This has been an agreeable surprise. It has helped to convince me that parents can be right on some subjects. And that is a very comforting thought in my present status.

While Father was enjoying himself teasing his Prohibitionist friends, some of them were having their own fun out of him. There was an old Baptist minister, in particular, who seemed to be strangely fascinated by Father. This old man, whom I shall call Arthur Edwards, was tall and angular and he always wore a long-tailed coat. He had small, quick eyes that shone like the buttons on a new pair of spats. His nose was long and thin and it overhung an extremely wide, thin-lipped mouth; but he could stretch his wide mouth into the most humorous grin I ever saw in my life. Mr. Edwards was literally Father's Boswell. He followed Father around and reported everything he did and said, even though he did not put his observations into writing. And nothing my father said ever insulted him. He grinned with increased delight at every new prodding and he always came back for more. Father liked Mr. Edwards, I know, for he always spoke of him with affection. But why Mr. Edwards liked Father I do not know. I suppose that Father went

on Bernard Shaw's assumption that people love to
be insulted.

Mr. Edwards was always pretending to be trying
to convert Father to Prohibition:

"Brother Yancey, you ought to join the ranks of
the Prohibitionists. All good Christian people belong."

"I have heard a lot about good Christian people,
but I never saw any."

"Well then, Brother Yancey, you ought to join
our ranks so you could get to Heaven. We will all
be there."

"I don't want to go to Heaven with a lot of
damned reformers. I'd prefer Hell—better company
down there with David and Voltaire. And surely
De Quincey will be in Hell, since dope fiends and
drunkards are in the same condemnation."

"Brother Yancey, you can't be serious. I see you
are not in the mood for discussing serious matters
today."

"I am serious. But you never are. You grin like a
God-damned Cheshire cat every time you come anywhere near me."

"Why, brother, aren't you afraid to take the Lord's
name in vain? The fear of God is the beginning of
wisdom."

"Yes, the beginning of wisdom. But the love of

God is its only worthy end: Fear denies love, and love wipes out fear."

"Well, at that, I am sure you are not serious when you suggest that God would damn a harmless Cheshire cat."

"I am not referring to my own God. I am just helping out the Baptist God who is always looking around for something else to damn."

Something like this went on whenever Mr. Edwards and Father got together. And they got together rather often, for wherever Father was, gravity seemed to pull Mr. Edwards in that direction.

Father had the most scandalous old hunting clothes. He bragged about the fact that he had used them for thirty-five years. Mother threatened all the time to burn them up but, instead, she kept on patching them because Father loved them so much. They had stains, which would not wash out, all over the enormous pockets, and the knees and the seats of the trousers were outrageously patched.

One night my father had returned from hunting and he stopped in a downtown restaurant to get a sandwich before going home. He had no sooner entered than in gravitated old Mr. Edwards.

"There now, Brother Yancey, you may say what you please, but I can tell from those patches on your knees that you are a good Christian."

Quick as a flash my father turned his back and pulled up his coat.

"If you look at my seat you will think I'm a hell of a backslider."

CHAPTER XII

Unmanageable Daughters

∿∿∿

AS I have said, my father was twenty years older than Mother. The women of Father's day were all ladies. It was through Father's own interest in sports that his daughters had become tomboys. But in spite of that fact, when we reached the age of fifteen or sixteen he expected us, miraculously, to transform into nice decorous little ladies. However, we didn't do that. The term "flapper" had just come into being, and we were flappers. Father could not get used to that word, flapper. It worried him all the time; and so did everything it implied.

The young ladies of father's day all learned embroidery, music and painting, but we had never been encouraged in any such accomplishments. Still, when childhood suddenly left us, Father was surprised that we did not immediately settle into those traditional ladylike pastimes. He began to take us in hand. He would not allow *his* daughters to become flappers.

My sister Elizabeth was selected to be the musician of the family. Music was just a pain in the neck to Elizabeth. She would use any excuse to escape her music lessons. And when the time came for daily practice she balked like a mule. However, she was not slow to find out that she could use the music to her own advantage, for Mother would allow her almost any privilege if only she would do her music. Elizabeth worked this racket on Mother for several years. Finally, her demands got to be so exorbitant that Mother gave up bribing her and Elizabeth gave up music.

When Elizabeth threw over music, she declared she wanted to study law. That was the only thing she was interested in, and that was what she was going to do. At this announcement my father almost had convulsions. He'd be damned if he would have any mannish women in his family; he would just be damned if he would allow it.

My mother said she did not see why he was so upset by Elizabeth's choice. He had always claimed that she was exactly like him. All of his people had been lawyers and, therefore, Elizabeth's decision was only natural.

"Well, none of the ladies in my family have ever been lawyers. My little daughter shall not study law either. I'll just be damned if I will pay her expenses for any such foolishness."

"Very well," said Elizabeth. "If you won't send me to law school, then I will get a job teaching school, and I will send myself."

"Go ahead," replied Father. He was perfectly sure that he had called her bluff.

But when Elizabeth did get a position to teach school Father raised the roof again. He next tried every persuasion. But Elizabeth remained firm in her resolve. Then, when Father saw that she would have her way regardless of threats and persuasion he, all at once, began to laugh about the whole thing. He'd be damned if he didn't believe she would make a success of her career too. The child was indeed exactly like himself.

But Elizabeth never did study law. She was married the very next year, which was more to my father's liking. But Mother didn't like her choice of matrimony any more than Father had liked her choice of a profession. She said Elizabeth was too young even to think of marriage. No girl of nineteen should take on the responsibilities of married life. Father laughed at this. He told my mother that the responsibilities of married life certainly sat lightly upon her shoulders.

Soon after Elizabeth's musical prelude had ended, Father decided to make me into an artist. He engaged a first-rate teacher for me and it was my business to go to her and be taught.

Father met with a little more success in my case because, as luck would have it, I really did like to paint. However, my great aptitude was for painting the wrong things. I made some mediocre progress with portraits and outdoor sketching. But then, having developed a passion for color combinations, I consumed all of my time and many gallons of paint in working out new schemes of decoration for my room. I painted my walls, woodwork, floor and even lovely old mahogany furniture four or five times every year, just to see what the effect would be. Of course, all this repainting involved, at times, a good deal of scraping with paint remover. But I never was one to quail in the face of manual labor.

Father disapproved of all this furniture painting and wall painting. He had not expected my genius to take such an utilitarian turn. He told me if I did not stop spending so much money on house paint he would just have to buy my colors himself. Damn it, this was the limit. Here he was expecting a bill for a few tubes of artist's colors and a little turpentine each month; and instead of that, the items were gallons of house paint, with quantities of paint remover and enormous brushes besides. He had never authorized me to buy turpentine in five-gallon cans.

At sixteen I was anything but the gentle young

portrait painter that Father had hoped I would be. Still, with all his protests against the undesirable by-products of my education in art, he was very proud of my pictures. Father had met with such unqualified defeat in his musical aspirations for Elizabeth, that a poor success with me was better than none at all. He loved to have me exhibit my pictures, if ever any of his friends were unguarded enough to show a spark of interest when he mentioned my remarkable talent.

My room faced that side of Lynchburg which overlooks the bluffs above James River. The view from my window was lovely—sheer cliffs bordering the river, topped by the thick green trees of Madison Heights—and beyond them the blue, irregular line of Candler's Mountains. Then Father bought his first automobile and he built the garage under my window.

The garage did not obstruct my view, but the ugly dark grey of the roof made a flat, colorless spot which I did not enjoy. One of the most beautiful sights in the world, I thought, is the deep red ploughed fields of Bedford County against the blue of the mountains: I would buy myself some deep red paint and I would change the garage roof to suit my own taste. I would transport Bedford County to Lynchburg. It may be that this was a somewhat unsophisticated idea for exterior decoration. However, at that time, I felt it would be deeply satisfying to my soul.

The day I painted the garage roof was the very day that Father happened to bring a perfectly strange man home with him. And, as usual, Father worked the conversation around to the artist in the family. But I did not know this until later.

I had rooted out an old pair of trousers belonging to my brother Joe. I had secured a ladder and I was having the time of my life painting the roof. My clothes were smudged all over with red paint, my face was splashed and splattered, and my arms and hands were a sight. In the midst of such great happiness I became aware of a conversation going on in the house. Father was talking to someone. I could not tell who it was. Then I heard quite clearly:

"Where is Rebecca, Joe?"

"She is out on top of the garage."

Silence. Then Father said, "She must be painting the view of the river. She loves that."

Silence again. Then I heard Father's decisive voice saying, "Tell Rebecca to come here."

I, at once, jumped to the conclusion that Joe had told Father I was painting the roof.

"The mean snake!" I thought. "Now I'll catch it for buying all this paint." Furiously I dipped out a large brushful of red paint and slapped it back and forth on the roof. The color was realistic enough to satisfy my instinct for revenge. I ground it into the tin.

Joe came to the window: "Beck, Father wants you."

"What does he want?" I snapped.

"He wants you. Hurry."

I got up off my haunches and scrambled down the ladder. At this Joe recognized his trousers and yelled out:

"Hey! What are you doing in my pants? I was saving those pants to wear fishing."

I paid no attention to him. With my mind busily manufacturing excuses for my extravagance, I hurried up the back steps. Joe had posted himself at the back door and he grabbed me as I attempted to slide past him.

"Give me my pants," he said, vehemently shaking me.

"Let me alone. I've got other worries," I retorted with withering scorn. I was determined I wouldn't be shorn of the pants before I had made my plea for art's sake.

But Joe didn't wither. "Give me my pants," he repeated. "I don't want 'em all messed up with paint."

"Why did you have to tell Father I was painting that roof?"

"I didn't tell him anything."

140

"You did. I heard you talking together. Why else would he want me?"

"He wasn't talking to me. He was talking to——."

I did not wait to hear Joe out. I gave him a quick kick on the shins. I pulled myself violently out of his clutches and went racing into the library with such speed that I almost crashed into Father, who stood just inside the door talking to a gentleman whose extremely dignified presence took away what little breath I had left.

Father was outraged by my appearance.

"Why—my dear little lady—in pants! What is the meaning of this?"

I was obliged to make my plea for art in front of this dignified stranger, in pants, and with my face speckled all over with red paint. Then I had to show my pictures which, of course, was the reason Father had had me called. The dignified stranger was quite nice about my pictures. He said everything that was expected of him, and more. He told my father that he was indeed fortunate in having a daughter so versatile that she could paint a roof, very good portraits and—with a bow to me—even improve on the lily as well.

I considered myself dismissed. But such gallantry from the dignified presence sent me flying off to a mirror to see whether, after all, it might not be very becoming if one happened to have natural freckles. It was possible that freckles might be as alluring as the spots on a veil, I thought; I must investigate.

Such powerful effect does a compliment have upon a sixteen-year-old that I even went to Joe and apologized for having misjudged him and for having kicked his shins. I promised him that if he would only let me keep his pants on a little longer, I would get every spot of paint out of them with some remover I had. Having made my peace with Joe, I hastened off to finish the roof, for the germs of reformation were at work and I had a feeling, besides, that Father was going to have something to say to me when his guest departed.

I was not mistaken. Father had his speech all prepared. But, much to my surprise, he did not censure me for my wastefulness in the matter of the red paint: I was supposed to be a young lady. I was being given lessons in art in recognition of the fact that it was time for me to acquire gentleness and modesty. It was a deep shock to come home with a distinguished friend and to find the little daughter he was so proud of dressed in her brother's old pants, painting the garage roof.

For some time after my experience with roof-painting, I tried to cultivate dignity, and nobody's pants were a temptation to me. I can not tell whether this change was due more to my father's unexpectedly gentle reproof, or to the gallantry of his distinguished friend. However, my reformation never amounted to even so much as well-glued-on veneer. Dignity just wasn't in the air at that time.

In the first place, it was the dances. When I first went to dancing school I had begun on the sedate waltz and two-step. But suddenly the dances went very muscular. They resembled a football scrimmage. I had a good set of pliable muscles, thanks to my father's early training, and I could easily manage all the queer gyrations that went by the name of "the new dances." I had plenty of endurance too. In fact I was inexhaustible. None of this made for dignity.

Then there was a posture called the "debutante slouch." That did not make for dignity either. The young ladies of Father's day were taught to sit and stand erect. It was considered very vulgar for a lady to touch the back of her chair when she sat, or to bend forward at all in walking. When the "debutante slouch" came in I took great pains to school my strong young muscles to this novel position. It took hours in front of a mirror. You had to throw one foot forward and bend that knee a little. Then you had to droop your shoulders with an air of nonchalance, and you flattened your derrière by poking out your stomach a tiny bit. Not too much. I had to practice this a long time before I got it down pat. One day, after I thought I had acquired the perfect posture, I noticed Father looking at me with a startled expression.

"Good God, Becky! Child," he said in a troubled voice, "have you hurt your spine?"

With great condescension I explained to Father that nothing was wrong with my spine. This was the stylish way to stand. It was the "debutante slouch."

"Well," said my father, "it looks more like the washtub hunch to me. I'll be damned if you don't look deformed. Please throw yourself back in joint when you come around me. I can't stand such contortions."

Perhaps it was the dresses, after all, that made dignity most impossible for me. Skirts suddenly hit a new high, and evening dresses turned sleeveless and neckless at the same time. Father stormed around for days after I appeared in my first sleeveless, neckless and practically skirtless evening dress. It was uncivilized, he said. He didn't see how Mother could allow it. A respectable woman permitting her daughter to go out in nothing more than a fig leaf!

But twenty years can make quite a difference in a person's point of view. My mother said if all the other girls my age were flappers he would just have to make up his mind that I would flap too.

"That damned word again!" said my father. "It

144

gives me hydrophobia just to hear it! If I gape like an imbecile for an expression, I *never* intend to add that odious word to my vocabulary!"

While all the tumult about flapperism was going on in our own home, we found out that Father had come to terms with it on the outside.

That year Father was toastmaster for the annual banquet of the alumni of the University of Virginia, and he had engaged a famous orator to make the address of the evening. This speaker had been intensively advertised in the papers, his subject had been announced, and the alumni were looking forward to hearing something quite outstanding. But after all the to-do, the much-heralded orator made such a short speech that it was over before his audience had really settled down to listen. Then Father arose to thank him and he added a few remarks of his own. He begged the indulgence of the gathering for taking up so much time himself. He was obliged to fill in because their illustrious guest had made his speech so unforgivably brief. That speech was like a flapper's dress: There was enough of it to cover the main points but it was so short it was downright disgraceful.

That the speaker for the alumni dinner was far from offended at Father's little joke was proven, a few days later, by the way in which we happened to find Father out. One afternoon the postman left

at our house a small squarish package addressed to
Father, and when he came home that evening, the
entire family stood around the library table watching while he opened the package up. Inside, wrapped
daintily around with white tissue, was the most
adorable little china doll! She had real hair and her
dimpled arms were outstretched in the most win-
ning manner. She had on no clothes at all except
the merest ruffle of a skirt, which did not even pretend to cover her rosy little behind. Over the bare
upper part of her body was stretched a narrow pink
ribbon, slantwise, from shoulder to waist. The ribbon was tied at the back in the most impudent little
bow imaginable, and across the front of it was
printed the single word, "Flapper." A card was
stuck in the paper which surrounded the little doll,
and the message written on it in neat style said:

"Just to prove to you that your criticism of my
speech was gross exaggeration." The card was not
signed. My father began to chuckle.

Everyone fell in love with the little doll at once.
Everyone except Mother. She said:

"Whoever sent you that thing must have been
drunk in Atlantic City." Then my father's chuckle
turned into a laugh. There was nothing for him to do
but explain to Mother why the doll had been sent.

"Well, I like that!" teased my mother when Father had finished his confession. "I thought I heard

you say that you *never* intended to add that odious word 'flapper' to your vocabulary!"

"I didn't intend to," answered Father, still laughing, "but necessity is the smother of intention."

CHAPTER XIII

Driving for Father

wwv

AFTER my brother Joe went to West Point to school, the job of family chauffeur fell upon my shoulders, and it was most inconvenient at times. My father was always wanting to go to the farm to see about planting the garden or something. Any excuse to get to the farm. He adored the country, but I was at an age when nothing looked so good to me as the city streets.

When Father got his feet in Bedford County it was almost impossible to drag him away. No matter if I had the most important engagement in town, he would not hurry. He loved to wander around the farm and I would trail behind him, hoping with every step I took that he would notice my wistful look and make his business snappy. But that never happened. For a fact, Father did not always have business. He just had a desire to be in the country and I was the goat, because he couldn't drive the car.

It was perfectly useless for me to follow Father around. Dogging his footsteps did no good. He was not even aware of my presence; but I never gave up hope. Off he would go to the barn, with me behind him. He would poke around in the harness or inspect the horses' stalls. Then he would go out to the garden. I came too. He looked up and down the rows of vegetables and examined the raspberry bushes and the grapevines. Next, he would stroll over to Uncle Jake's cabin. I shadowed him. He would engage Uncle Jake in a long conversation about the cows and calves or the hogs. I would stand first on one foot and then on the other, debutante slouch forgotten.

As likely as not, Father would leave Uncle Jake's to go rambling off to the most remote cornfield. Ah —here was something that gave him real pleasure! The further the better. He had a very characteristic way of taking off his hat and walking along in the sunshine. He would throw back his head and shoulders and, with an expression of perfect happiness, he seemed to be drinking in the rays of the sun. This habit of Father's is hard to describe. There was such an attitude of peace and joy and almost reverence about it that it left one feeling it was an act of worship.

149

After Father had spent ages meandering all over the farm, he would suddenly look at his watch and demand that I get going immediately. He had promised to meet a client at his office at five—or something equally as important to him. I had been itching to go for hours; but he never suggested such a thing until long after it was too late for me to do anything about what I had on my mind. Just the same, he was all at once in a great hurry to get back to Lynchburg. He would start off toward the house almost at a gallop. It was all I could do to keep up with him.

The difficulties of driving twenty years ago were much greater than they are today. Very few of the roads in Virginia were paved, and you could travel for miles and miles without seeing a filling station. If we got stuck in the mud, or had a flat tire, my father was as helpless as a baby. Although he could waste hours at the farm, pottering around at nothing, when he got ready to travel he wanted plenty of action. Nothing irritated him so much as any kind of delay. He simply couldn't understand why such a thing should happen to him.

I could get a car out of the mud as well as any man, but this took time, and it never occurred to Father to fall to and help. He had grown up with horses. They were trained to obey commands, and he could not see why an automobile wouldn't do the same thing. Whenever we got stuck in the red clay of Bedford County my father would leap nimbly to the grass at the side of the road. From there he employed the tactics of the wise man who did the grunting while his fellow did the work. I would find sticks and branches and push them under the wheels for a staying power; then I would jump back into the seat and start the engine buzzing. When the car began sawing away my father would begin yelling at it:

"Get out of that damned mud hole, damn it!"

The automobile didn't obey Father's orders. Like the tar-baby, it just didn't pay any attention to him, at which he would roar out louder:

"Get to hell out of that damned mud, I say, damn it!"

Father's exhortations never helped. Eventually, I got out of the mud in spite of them, and I even believe I could have gotten out without them. Nevertheless, they made Father feel that he was doing his bit. When finally we were out of the mud, he would climb back to his place with an air of supreme self-satisfaction.

I had learned to jack up a car, patch an inner tube, and replace a tire in a reasonable length of time. But to Father, standing helpless on the roadside, the necessity for such a delay was nothing but a vicious scheme of automobile manufacturers to encroach

151

upon his time. He would pronounce curses upon the makers of all automobiles for fashioning tires that got punctures, and he called upon high heaven to witness the injustice to himself. One day he wound up his harangue with a "damn it to hell, these things are an infernal nuisance!"

Just then my knuckles went "crack" against a lug I was screwing on.

"Damn it to hell, they *are*," I affirmed with conviction.

Father jumped as if he had been shot.

"Oh, my dear little girl," he said in a shocked voice, "don't use such language. Men swear. Little ladies don't swear."

I flung my wrench crashing into the tool box. "I have a man's work to do," I flared back.

"That was probably the excuse of Catherine the Great," returned Father shortly.

I could hardly wait to get back to Lynchburg and look up all I could find about Catherine.

After I had done this, Father's terse warning grew teeth.

Anyone would think that in the summer, when we moved to the country, my chauffeuring job would have been easier. Bedford was where Father wanted to be, and there he was. But it wasn't easier. It was more complicated than ever, for Father had to go to town to his office every morning.

In the days when we had only horses, it had been Uncle Jake's duty to go to and from the station with Father each day. Father loved to drive his own horses, so Uncle Jake only went along to drive the buggy when Father wasn't in it.

When we were little children, the biggest event of any day was to be allowed to drive the three miles to the station in the morning when Father caught the train. If we begged hard enough, and had not gotten into any particular mischief, the family carriage was hitched up for the occasion and several of us could go. But there were so many children that we had to take turns and, if the carriage went out in the morning, it was an unwritten law that it had to go back in the evening when Father came home again. This was to furnish an outing for those children who had been left out on the first trip.

The evening trips were very nice, especially if we could persuade Uncle Jake to go early, for then we could get candy at Mr. Lindsay's cross-roads store; and the candy at Lindsay's was wonderful—different from any we ever saw in town. There were lumps of bright pink "French" candy, which were shaped like rosettes; and these tasted a little like tooth paste. Then there were long, orange-colored marshmallow things called "banana candy." They were flavored with banana oil and their shape was quite realistic. And of course there were ropes of licorice "shoe strings." Altogether, buying candy at Lindsay's was a pleasant experience, and we considered ourselves fortunate indeed if Uncle Jake could be coaxed into taking us over early. After we had met Father's train there was no chance of any of us going into Lindsay's store.

Father sometimes went into Lindsay's himself and, when he did, he usually stayed a long time. But he would not let any of us get out of the carriage to buy candy. He said the candy we liked was "horrible stuff—enough to give you ten straight weeks of colic." Generally, though, Father himself did not stop at Lindsay's store. As a rule, he was in a hurry to get home; and the only thing he really liked to stop for was to talk to the Italians.

These Italians were laborers who were engaged in widening the railroad bed and laying a double track. In the evening, when Father's train got in, they had usually just stopped work, and they would be swinging jauntily up the road—sometimes singing snatches of song in unison. Father would always stop and talk to them, and they would stand chattering, gesticulating and laughing with volatile animation. I could not understand a word that was being said, but I could tell from the Italians' expressions that they were all having a grand time. And Father was as pleased with them as they were with him. It was these Italians who helped to make the trips to the station in the morning far more desirable than the ones at night.

Father could time the arrival of the train at Forest Depot perfectly. He never figured on leaving our house one minute sooner than it would take him to roll up to the station just as the train pulled in. The train only stopped at Forest for three minutes. But Father knew his horses. And we all knew that if we happened to cross the bridge at Lindsay's store one second later than the train went under it there was small chance of Father's getting to Lynchburg. From the bridge on, it was a race between the train and Father's horses. This was delightfully thrilling, and it happened every morning.

Down the road we would come at a brisk trot, fringe of the carriage dancing; three tense children on the back seat, and Uncle Jake at Father's side, as immovable as a lump of mahogany; Father, alert for the moment when the train's whistle should blow for the curve above the bridge. Then the sound of the whistle would split the air! Both train and carriage had five hundred yards to go before reaching the bridge. Now was Father's chance to show off his horsemanship! But the horses needed very little urging. They understood the signal of the whistle. They were as excited as we were. Flying like the wind, our carriage would strike the bridge just as the train plunged under it. Great billows of black smoke rose up in our faces. Dashing across the bridge we would go, and down the level road which led to the station. As we went past the old post office, where the Italians were at work, they would drop their shovels and, jumping up and down and wildly waving their arms about, they would yell out things at Father. I do not know what the Italians said, for my knowledge of their language is limited to a few elementary words. But I have a feeling that they were quite partisan and unconventional because, every now and then as we sped along, my father would send a darting glance in their direction and laugh as if he would burst. And his face, as he did this, would take on that impish expression which men and small boys have when they are involved in some discussion not meant for feminine ears.

All of this hue and cry would cause the passengers on the train to poke their heads out of the windows. Then they would wave their hands and begin to cheer us on. When finally, at the station, Father drew up his horses almost on their haunches, people would come rushing out to the platform and laughingly welcome Father onto the train. He had made it again! The Italians up the tracks now broke into uproarious applause. All we lacked was a brass band.

It was habits of this kind that made driving for Father in Bedford so trying. He had to have some sort of excitement to get him off to Lynchburg in a victorious mood. After he bought an autombile it was no fun racing with the train. It lacked the sporting interest. People do not notice an automobile speeding along the highway. It is not at all spectacular. Besides that, Father never really got used to speed in an automobile. It always alarmed him a little. And so he had to work out a new plan for projecting a morning conquest.

Father only got his new plan perfected after Joe had left for West Point, and at first I did not see through his design. He continued to get up early in the morning, and his standing orders to Aunt Nancy were that breakfast was to be at seven o'clock, as usual. But, after breakfast, he would waste a solid hour or more giving Uncle Jake perfectly useless orders about what he wanted him to do that day. Not only that. When Father left the breakfast table, he expected Uncle Jake, without any prearrangement, to be stationed and waiting on the identical spot where his work was to take place, so that he could show him *how* he wanted it done.

Sometimes when Father got up from the table he would go straight to the barn. If Uncle Jake was not there, Father would stand in his tracks and roar at the top of his voice:

"Jake! Jake! Damn it, where is that fellow Jake? Come here, Jake, you will get me left by that damned train."

Again, Father would make straight for the garden and, if Uncle Jake did not at once appear, as if by magic, the same accusations would come sailing back to the house on the morning breeze. My father had a marvelous pair of lungs, and nobody could plausibly claim not to have heard him the first time he called—unless he happened to be five miles away. However, that did not keep Father from calling again and yet again. He kept up a continual clamor until Uncle Jake came loping into view.

While all this fuss was going on, the whole family would be gathered on the porch, waiting to see Father off for the day. After so long a time, Mother would reach down in her bag of tricks and pull out the voice that laid all of her husband's faults at the door of his children:

"Your father just can't get off to town with any feeling of satisfaction until he has left everybody behind him in a state of excitement," she would remark. Then as Father kept up his importunities, she would add:

"Why on earth doesn't that impossible man send word to Uncle Jake, while he is at breakfast, where he wants to meet him?"

None of us attempted to answer this riddle. Father himself did not know where he would want Uncle Jake to be. If he happened to go to the swimming pond, and saw anything that needed attention, he just wanted Uncle Jake down there instantly. That was all there was to it. Uncle Jake had been carrying out his orders ever since he was a boy, and Father knew he would obey his instructions more faithfully than anyone else. At the same time, the swimming pond was a good distance from the house, and under a rather steep hill. Father never did find Uncle Jake down there. Nevertheless, he was always annoyed when he didn't.

In fact, Uncle Jake would usually be in the kitchen, which was, of course, in a little building outside the house. There he would sit in the doorway, quietly singing "Swing Low, Sweet Chariot" and patting his foot to keep time to the music, until the atmosphere rang with his summons. If the command came from the direction of the pond, Uncle Jake would have to do quite a lot of hurrying to get there in time to prevent Father from going up in spontaneous combustion.

On cool mornings Uncle Jake would be dozing by the kitchen stove, and then Aunt Nancy would have to arouse him when his orders came through.

"Jake," she would say, shaking with laughter and pulling at Uncle Jake's arm, " Jake, git up f'om dar. Don't you hear Gawd A'mighty callin' you?"

During preliminary skirmishes, I would have put the automobile in position near the side of the front porch. At eight o'clock, promptly, I would take my place at the wheel and there I would sit. But it was only after Father had wasted enough time to make it impossible for him to catch the train that he would come dashing up at top speed, and calling out light-hearted good-byes to his assembled family. Jumping into the car, and slamming the door with a loud bang, he would announce that we were sure to miss that damned train if I didn't hurry! Off I would start in an already hopeless attempt.

As I have said, I did not immediately see through my father's subterfuge. I really believed he wanted to make the train. I took myself a bit seriously, and to get dressed to take Father to Forest Depot was a vastly different affair from making a toilet sufficiently elaborate to appear on the streets of Lynchburg. The first time we missed the train and I was forced to drive up in front of the Kall Building, dressed in an old khaki middy suit, my ego was terribly deflated. It was just at the time of the morning when all the young men I knew were coming downtown to their offices. I did not have on even a smudge of powder or lipstick. This made me feel absolutely nude, for it was a year when all the girls my age were wearing extremely white noses and rather red lips.

After a few such experiences, I was thoroughly wise to Father, and I was always prepared. Instead of sitting dutifully at the wheel, waiting for him to appear, I was occupied with a campaign of my own. I would put on one of my nicest dresses and get my hair up in style. This left almost an hour for me to experiment to my own satisfaction with powder and lipstick. By the time Father made his sprint for the car, I had completed quite a job of camouflage, and I was ready for the inevitable.

My father was not accustomed to finding his chauffeuse in mask. The first time he steamed out and saw me thus properly geared up to enter the city of Lynchburg, he stopped short in his tracks a few paces from the car.

"Why in the hell do you have to put on all that war paint!" he demanded.

When we were in the country, my evening drive for Father could often be attended by as many unexpected complications as characterized the morning trip; for frequently our guests put Father to a great deal of inconvenience in the matter of transportation.

Father always had to come back to Bedford on the train, since I couldn't wait for him all day in town. If we had guests who were going to Lynchburg in the evening, we made one trip do for both. The hitch here was that Father's train from Lynchburg got in half an hour before the arrival of the train going to Lynchburg. Naturally, we had to make Father wait the half-hour, rather than dump our guests down to sit in a barren country station, and this always vexed Father. He hated to wait for anything. When he got ready to go he expected to go, then and there. But one time I made him wait to the limit of his endurance.

I was taking my best beau over to catch the train back to Lynchburg, and of course we were in no hurry to get to the station. As we approached Lindsay's store there stood my father, peering up the road. He had walked that far and he didn't look the picture of patience. I dared not stop. I called out strategically, in passing, that I would be right back. I would just leave John at the train, which was almost due then. But the train was late. This was something that had never been known to happen before. . . . Somehow I didn't start back for Father until John's train had come in.

The evenings in Bedford County get very chilly toward the end of August. When finally I got back to Lindsay's my father was sitting on a bench in front of the store and, except for his face, I could not have recognized him. He had waited and waited, and he was "cold as hell." So he had gone into the store and had gotten Mr. Lindsay to give him yards and yards of wrapping paper and some cord. Then he had wrapped his legs in paper and tied them up with string. He looked like Buffalo Bill in paper chaps. He did not like it at all when I sat down on the bench and laughed at him. He was tired, and he was "damned near frozen" from having been forced to wait so long.

However, Father's long wait was not ended yet, for when we got to the car I saw that a tire was flat. This was almost more than Father could bear. He gave vent to his feelings in an explosion of damns against automobiles and cold nights and late trains, and especially against damned half-baked boys who interfered with his evening's peace and comfort. Then suddenly, in the midst of his tirade, Father took cognizance of a number of countrymen who stood around inside of Lindsay's store. He now saw a way to speed up our departure! Just as I was preparing to get out the tools and jack up the wheel his mood changed.

"Now, my dear child, there is no need for you to do that," said my father.

Quite unconscious of his rustling paper pants, Father strode over to the entrance of the store. He flung open the screen door.

"Gentlemen," he proclaimed, "my little daughter is out here changing a tire and I am sure all of you would want to help her."

Six stout yokels poured out of the store, eager to aid the damsel in distress, and my father, crackling like a log fire on Christmas day, took instant command of these reinforcements. He even knew their first names.

"Now, Paul," he instructed, "you jack up that wheel. Jim, you be unscrewing those lugs while Bill gets the spare tire off; and Frank, you can get out the pump."

All hands seemed perfectly willing to obey orders. I had nothing to do but stand and look on.

After our fresh tire had been speedily screwed in place Father was ready with further directions:

"Here, Pete, these boys have done their part. You take a turn at pumping."

Pete at once leaped to the job.

"Now, Ralph, you pump a while, and let Pete rest."

Ralph never questioned his authority and, in short order, all was quite ready. As soon as I was in my seat, my father climbed, crackling, into the car.

"Thank you, gentlemen; thank you very much," he bowed cordially. "I hope I can assist you in the same way some day."

All the gentlemen seemed perfectly charmed with the whole performance from beginning to end.

And I was left wondering. I will pass over Father's offer of future assistance to our willing helpers. But I did wonder how he could know the exact procedure by which the changing of a tire could best be expedited, when he had never even tried to change one in his life!

CHAPTER XIV

On Appreciating Father

wwww

FATHER had friends and relations all over Virginia and he never forgot a one of them. Whenever any one of us was going away to spend even so much as a week-end, he would demand about ten of our visiting cards and on them he would write messages to his friends and relatives in that town. No matter what our hostesses had planned for our entertainment, we had to find time to call upon the elderly people for whom these cards were intended. When we came home again, we had to make a report to Father about how they had looked, and what they had said. Especially what they had said about him. Some of the people to whom we had to pay our respects were actually the mothers and fathers of men and women Father's own age. They were old enough to be our great-grandparents, but my father

165

had visited in their homes as a boy, and he wanted them to know us. They had nothing in common with us, and I imagine we must have bored them most desperately. However, it never occurred to Father that this might be the case. He assumed that anyone who had ever known him would certainly be interested in his children. Even if he himself had not seen them for fifty or sixty years, he was perfectly sure they would welcome us with pure unadulterated joy.

This peculiarity of Father's overcast every trip I ever had. Whenever I went anywhere it was always with a feeling of acute rebellion at the thought of those visiting cards in my purse. They were like tentacles pulling at me when I wanted to be gay and carefree.

My mother had an older brother who was an officer in the regular army. At the time of the World War, he was stationed at Camp Grant, which was about sixty miles from Chicago, near Rockford, Illinois. During Christmas of 1917, my mother's brother and his wife were visiting in Lynchburg. They had no children and, when their furlough was nearly over, they suggested that I be allowed to return with them to Rockford as a companion for my aunt, since my uncle had to live at camp. My mother thought this would be a lovely trip for me.

We started for Chicago soon after Christmas. I

had never been so far away from home before. It was the first time I had ever left Lynchburg without a bunch of visiting cards inscribed with messages to Father's friends and relations and, inwardly, I was rejoicing that at last I was going somewhere free and unencumbered. No old ladies and gentlemen to visit! None of Father's friends to bother with! What joy! But I soon found out that Father was inescapable.

My uncle was expecting to be ordered to France at any moment and although he and my aunt had been married for years and years, they were rediscovering all sorts of attractions in each other. They paid no attention to me. The train was crowded, on account of so many people going here and there: to camps to see their boys before they left for "Over There"; to Washington to see if they could hatch out a commission in the army; and to any convenient place for a wedding rendezvous. When we entered the first Pullman there was only one vacant seat. My aunt and uncle wanted to be more private. They left me installed in the vacant seat and they went to the next car in search of a whole compartment for themselves.

I observed that I was sharing the compartment with a very nice-looking man who seemed to me, at that time, quite middle-aged and I saw that he was a Jew. Having settled this, without further thought of my fellow-traveler, I took out some magazines and proceeded to entertain myself for a considerable time.

I had never possessed any handsome luggage, but this Christmas I had received a very nice overnight bag which was marked with my initials. There it was at my feet where I had left it when I had opened it for the magazines. The lettering was turned outward: "R.V.Y., LYNCHBURG, VA."

All during the time I was reading, I was vaguely conscious of the fact that my companion was giving me an interested glance at decent intervals. This did not bother me—but I was aware of the man's scrutiny and, after a while, I happened to look up from my book straight into his eyes. They were large black eyes—very grave; there was nothing forward about them. It seemed rather natural when my vis-à-vis said:

"If your name is Yancey, I think I have spent the night at your home."

Of course "Y" is an unusual initial. There are few names with this initial in any city, so my companion's remark did not seem a startling deduction. However, I owe it to myself to explain why I happened to become involved in a conversation with this perfectly strange man.

In the first place, I must go into Virginia traditions, and then comes my inescapable Father.

I suppose nothing seems so ridiculous to other people as our peculiar form of Virginia ancestor-worship. But the thing has its uses. We must all have some kind of standard by which to judge people. Virginians are essentially lazy, and their ancestor-worship prevents much unnecessary mental exertion. If one recognizes from a person's name, for instance, that he comes from a family which for generations has stood for the best traditions, then one can safely make a friend of that person without bothering any further. If he turns out to be a thief and a blackguard it will be the exception, not the rule. And one won't make many mistakes.

I can illustrate with the Lee family, which is more or less a public possession, and therefore all right to use. If you happen to run into anyone on a train whom chance identifies as one of the Virginia Lees, you know, without thinking, that this person will be honorable and gentle and courteous. He will almost certainly be a person of culture, and he will stand for the highest principles: Father used to say the most truly great of all Virginians was a Lee.

Well, I now found myself, by chance, opposite this friendly middle-aged man. He was unmistakably a descendant of Abraham, whom I had been taught to admire. I didn't need to be told who his ancestors were. His traditions were somewhat older and more widely known than those of the Lees: He would not steal my purse. He would not try to lure me down the primrose path. And, since he would not bear false witness against his neighbor, he would never publish it abroad that I was a person of easy virtue simply because I had indulged in an innocent conversation without proper introduction. Besides, he represented a race to which I was under heavy obligation: Father was always cautioning us to remember that the greatest benefactor of all mankind was a Jew.

My father had definite ideas on all subjects. I knew what to think about Jews without any effort at all. "Jews," Father had often said, "Jews are the only real Christians. They are the only people I see forgiving their enemies and turning the other cheek. This is true of them because Christianity is the flower of their culture, whereas with us it is only grafted on. Yet we have forced this proud people into a position where they have repudiated their own heritage." Then Father would add, "You have got to admire a race that has produced such men as Moses, David, Jesus, Spinoza, Disraeli—" Father would fire out a long list. "And you've got to make many allowances for a race so intense that they executed Jesus because they admired Him."

I never got very far with this last observation of Father's. I would start with "admiration—envy—feeling of inferiority—fear—then hate with dire consequences—followed by a terrible defensive regret down through the ages—defensiveness exaggerated by persecution—compensating how?—" Here my thoughts would trail off. I didn't know what Father meant.

But thus it was partly because of Father that I began talking to this stranger on the train. He was almost like an old friend. I was sure he was a gentleman.

"When did you spend the night at our house?" I inquired. "I don't remember it."

"You were just a little girl. It was in Bedford County."

"It has been a long time since I was a little girl," I answered, proud of my imposing age.

"Well, then, it was in 1908. I came to America in 1907. I went to Lynchburg, where I had relatives. I did not know much English, and the best I could do was to peddle small articles all through the counties.

"One day in the summer of 1908 I came up to the gate of a lovely old brick house. It had a huge lawn around it. There was a very beautiful lady sitting on the porch and she was reading a book."

I laughed here. "That couldn't have been anyone but Mother," I said.

"Yes, it was," continued my friend. "And there was a man in the yard who was making a bench. His back was turned to me. He was hammering on the bench."

Again I interrupted with a laugh. "It must have been Sunday," I edged in. But this facetious remark was entirely overlooked.

"I came up the drive with my pack on my back, and then the man turned and saw me. He glared at me fiercely:

" 'Don't you know it's against the law to peddle goods in this county?' he asked. I began to make apologies and all at once he broke into the merriest laugh I ever heard in my life.

" 'Come on in,' he said, 'I was just joking. In Lynchburg I am an officer of the law, but out here, you can see for yourself, I am only a very poor carpenter.'

" 'Oh, you are Mr. Yancey, aren't you?' I asked, and of course it was your father. Naturally your family were not interested in what I had in my pack. But they let me talk to the servants and I sold a good many things. And I stayed to supper and spent the night. I never was so kindly treated."

"And I will bet," I here remarked, "that you did your kind deed too. For I am sure you didn't escape having to admire Father's engineering jobs—his swimming pond that he makes over every year, his wonderful, homemade shower bath; and the hydraulic ram which is supposed to supply our house with water. That is his pet hobby. He loves for it to break so he can mend it."

My companion looked at me with large, somber eyes, full of oriental disapproval at my lack of parental respect.

"I think you underrate your father," he said. "It is a wonderful thing for a man who carries his large responsibilities to have such diverting hobbies. His work must be disillusioning in the extreme—dealing with criminals all day as he does. Yet he is as simple and wholesome as a child."

In those days a girl reached for her Dorin instead of a cigarette to tide over an awkward moment. I took out my Dorin, and my friend continued with a slightly amused expression:

"I suppose you would naturally think, since I began with a pack on my back, that I am not in a position to say this, but I can tell you that your father is far ahead of his times, in many ways. I have read some of his reports to the city council, made during the time when he was Mayor, and you should, too. He understands more about engineering than you apparently think. I know this too: There is not a man of humble station in Lynchburg who is not sure that old Captain Bob is the champion of the poor."

"Oh," I said flippantly, "we are poor ourselves. And I suppose that any man who holds public office must do something for the people whose servant he is. Otherwise, he would not be elected."

My friend laughed now. "I see you are at an age which hates to be suspected of having serious thoughts," he commented slowly, but with such a kind and understanding expression that I forgot his reprimand.

By the time my new friend had left our train at Washington, I was half convinced that Father's family did not properly appreciate him. Later on I went the other half. This was after we had arrived at Camp Grant and I had met General K—— at my first ball in Rockford.

General K—— was a tall and very courtly old gentleman. He had whiskers like those of Chief Justice Hughes. He was a friend of my uncle's and he joined our group as we came into the ballroom. Then, as I was standing next to him when the music began, he asked me to dance.

"You know, you have a very unusual name," said General K——, sliding into the easy lame-duck which is customary with generals.

I agreed that my name was unusual.

"I have heard the name before, though," continued the General. "I have never forgotten the name because I have never forgotten the man I knew who had the name."

I asked the polite and obvious question.

174

"He was a very young man at the time I knew him," replied the General, lame-ducking along. "He was Mayor of a little town down in Virginia—most attractive fellow I ever saw—was Mayor of Lynchburg—named Robert Yancey. Did you ever know him?"

"Oh, yes, I know him. I live in his house," I answered frugally. Green as I was at an army post, I knew I should have to make this topic of conversation last through the whole dance, since no second lieutenant is going to cut in on a general.

We lame-ducked a few more paces.

"I imagine this Bob Yancey is your grandfather, then."

"No, he is my father." More lame-duck.

"He must have been married rather late in life."

"Yes—it was on account of rat poison that he married at all."

"Rat poison?" puzzled the General.

"Yes, Father had a colored man named Sam who——"

"Oh, I remember Sam," General K—— laughed. His lame-duck became quite spirited at this reminiscence of his youth.

"Well, then, you remember that Sam did everything but breathe for Father. Mother says that when Sam died Father had to get married, because he was so helpless."

The General laughed again. "But where did the rat poison come in?"

"Well, you see, Sam had indigestion one night. He went down to the kitchen to take some soda. But it turned out not to be soda.— When father and his bachelor friends found him it was too late to do anything about it."

"My—how awful!" said the General.

"Yes, it was. But, on the other hand, I probably wouldn't be here if it hadn't happened."

Our lame-duck ended with a sprightly limp as the music of "Take Me Back to Indiana" died a violent death. But the General and I became very good friends after that. It was all on account of Father, of course. The General seemed to get some sort of vicarious kick out of any tale about Father's unrestrained doings, and so gratifying is it to have an interested audience that, before every dance, I found myself preparing little dissertations for him: Father on outdoor exercise, Father on religion, Father in the courtroom.

It was a great pleasure to have the friendship of this distinguished old gentleman. I knew I could not claim any credit because of my own attractions and, after seven months at Rockford, I went back home with a feeling of consecration. I was resolved to be more thoughtful about doing things to show Father that I appreciated him.

When I got back to Virginia my family was in the country. Father was just ending his vacation and, as usual, he had spent his two weeks making improvements on the swimming pond.

But this year operations hadn't clicked off as usual. Father was due back at his office the next day and he had not yet completed his work on the pond to a point where the water could be turned in again. It was a damned shame, he said, the second shipment of cement had been late coming out to Bedford and this had delayed him. One more day would finish things out nicely. But he would be obliged to go back to town tomorrow, because he had some very important letters and papers to get off.

My mother had a typewriter which she had learned to use in order to facilitate her poetry writing, and she had acquired a fair amount of skill at typing. She said she would be perfectly willing to write Father's papers so that he could stay in the country another day.

That would not do, my father replied. If he was going to get the pond finished he had to be down there every minute. He could not stay at the house dictating to her and yet superintend his work in another place. He was not twins.

Mother ignored this hint. She said after all it would not matter so terribly much if the work on the pond waited until Saturday, when he would have a full day off from his office. "The thing has been dry for two weeks," she told him. "It won't kill anybody not to be able to swim for a few days more."

"That is easy for you to say because you don't use it," answered Father. "I hate for the children to be deprived of their pleasure any longer than is necessary."

Here I stepped in and "broke my molasses jug," as Uncle Remus says: I would go down to the pond and stay all day and write Father's papers. He could dictate to me while he directed his work.

Father was overjoyed at this.

"But you don't know how to use a typewriter," my mother demurred.

"If you will lend the typewriter, I will learn to-morrow," I returned, not daunted in the least. "I'll be slow, of course. But, if the pond takes part of Father's time, I ought to be able to keep up with him."

Father was satisfied that my plan would work splendidly. Accordingly, the next morning he got a huge stack of papers together while I went off with Mother to receive a rudimentary lesson in typewriting.

Mother was still quite doubtful about the arrangement.

"I hope you realize what you are getting yourself

into," she warned. "You know your father is not the most patient person in the world. He can be awfully exacting in his demands."

"Mother," I replied tartly, "it is a pity that nobody in his own family has any sympathy for Father's wholesome hobbies. His work must be disillusioning in the extreme—dealing with criminals all day as he does. You can thank his many hobbies for the fact that he is as simple and wholesome as a child, in spite of the large responsibilities he has to carry. I don't believe you appreciate what an unusual person he is. If you are not willing to do him a little favor, I *am*."

My mother looked at me with eyes like calm blue pools of water.

"I don't doubt," she answered in a sweet, perfectly even tone, "that I make a good many mistakes in handling a person of your father's charm and individuality. He is very fond of young people and I am sure that he will be happy and flattered to have your cooperation."

Feeling very righteous, I picked up a ream of paper and went off to join my father at the pond. Behind me came Uncle Jake and a young colored man named Ulysses S. Grant Poindexter who carried the typewriter, two chairs and a small table, and who were to help Father with his cement work.

All morning I sat on one of those hard-bottomed

chairs pecking laboriously away at the typewriter with one finger. Nothing could have been more boring than Father's papers. There were no details of any fascinating crimes divulged in them. The words I was so painfully picking out might as well have been Greek: "The party of the first part, the aforesaid plaintiff," "whereas the undersigned defendant"—not a word to take hold of my imagination or to inspire my zeal!

When I would lag behind, correcting a mistake or struggling to catch up with Father's rapid fire of unfamiliar words, he would get up from his chair and go over to give Ulysses S. Grant and Uncle Jake some close-range criticism. Then he would get so interested in what they were doing that he would take up a trowel and work a little himself. But if I caught up while he was doing this, it was no signal for me to relax. I tried it.

Once I wandered away under the trees, thinking to ease my boredom by inhaling the fragrance of some wild flowers that bordered the near-by brook. And when Father turned and saw my vacant chair he raised a great rumpus.

How could he finish the work he had to do if I did not stay where he could find me directly? It was the very devil for him to run two jobs at once and then to have to look for me as well. I would have to sit right in my chair where he could see me. It dis-

turbed his continuity of thought if he had to yell
all over the countryside for me when he was ready
to dictate. If I was going to make good my promise
to help him I would have to stick to my guns.

After that, I sat at attention when I was not writing.

We took an hour off for lunch and when we came
in to the table my mother was quite casual in her in-
quiries: How were we getting along with our work?

"We are doing nicely," answered Father. "We
have done more than I had expected. I think we'll
get through without any trouble."

"Without any trouble!" I thought ruefully. I had
had nothing but trouble since the day began. Still
I put on a cheerful front in Mother's presence. And
the food did me good. I went back to the pond with
renewed resolution.

But the afternoon dragged more heavily than the
morning. It was terribly hot. I was certainly not at-
taining any skill as a typist either. A group of un-
tried muscles between my shoulders ached with dull
fury as I pecked, erased, and pecked again.

The sweetest music I ever remember was hearing
Father say:

"Now—that is the last letter. You gather up the
papers neatly while I go over and check up on the
dam."

Everything was going fine. Uncle Jake took the typewriter and started up the path.

Father went to show Ulysses where to spread the last batch of cement. And that was what brought my day of appreciating Father to its climax. As Ulysses leaned over he dropped his hod and a big plop of cement splashed up in Father's eyes.

Father roared out in agony.

"Jake! Jake!" he wailed. "Good God, Jake! Come and get me. This damn fool has put out both my eyes!"

Uncle Jake sped to the assistance of his idol. He took Father's arm and led him up the hill. Laden with papers, I brought up the rear, sorrowfully solicitous of my father's suffering.

But Father was not content with the attention he was getting. While Uncle Jake was steering him along he continued to broadcast his affliction:

"Rosebud! Rosebud! For God's sake, come here! I am blind. That damned young fool has put out my eyes. By God, I am as blind as a bat!

"Rosebud, where are you? Why don't you hurry? Didn't you hear me say I am blind?"

As we approached the house my mother walked serenely down the drive to meet us. She put her arm around Father's shoulder as if he had been a little child.

"There, there," she reassured him, soothingly. "I

don't think you are blind. It is only the sand and lime that hurts. You will be all right."

Father, however, was not all right for quite a while. He refused to open his eyes. He insisted that the light would ruin them if they happened to have even a spark of eyesight left.

My mother made him lie down on his bed. She got a bowl of ice water in which she wet a towel, and she laid the cold, wet towel over Father's eyes. Then all the family came in to commiserate Father. Even in the midst of his travail he did not forget to give everyone a job. All of his children had to line up in his room and wring out cold towels so that he would not be a moment without one properly chilled. Mother was sent to crack more ice for the water, and I was dispatched to the station to get his letters off on the evening mail. It was a great day for Father.

When I got back from Forest my father was propped up in bed. He still had a wet towel over his eyes and my sister Mary was feeding him his supper, for he was still insisting that he was blind.

We had a doleful meal punctuated only by Father's groans, for he was enjoying himself far too much to let us forget his suffering. I expect he removed the towel, and satisfied himself that his eyesight was unimpaired, as soon as we had all gone to the dining room. But he was determined that we should not linger at the table unmindful of him and, when he thought we had been allowed enough time for supper, he demanded that we give him our undivided attention again.

By eight o'clock we were all exhausted. Mother went upstairs to her room. Henry straggled off to his own diversions. Caroline and I pulled two comfortable chairs to the coolest corner of the porch and flopped into them, leaving only Mary to minister to Father. Mary had more of Mother's gentleness than the rest of us, and she sat by Father's bedside, holding his hand.

We did not have a telephone in our house in the country and consequently we girls never made dates in advance. Sometimes several automobiles full of friends would appear during an evening; or a bunch of boys we knew would come over on horseback. Then for several evenings, perhaps, we would not see a soul but the family.

When Caroline and I flopped into our two chairs on the coolest corner of the porch, which incidentally was just outside Father's bedroom door, we were both fervently hoping that this would be one evening we should not have callers. We had not had time to dress. We were hot and tired, and we felt horrid. Hardly did our hopes find words for expression when the clatter of horses' hoofs came to our ears. There were several horses. They were coming up the near-by hill at a brisk trot. Caroline and I did not wait for further observations. We jumped from our chairs and shot through Father's room, announcing to Mary as we passed:

"Some boys are coming!"

Mary dropped Father's hand with a "plunk" and we all ran upstairs. Then all three of us stood hanging over the banister, calling to Father in very loud whispers:

"Tell them we have gone to bed!"

There was nothing for my father to do but forget his great affliction and to meet the visitors who had now drawn up their horses at the corner of the porch. Father was fully clothed. In his acute distress, he had only removed his shoes when first he had lain down, and now he could not find them in the dark. We heard him muttering as he fumbled for them, and finally he gave it up. We heard him go out to the porch, padding along in his stocking feet. Then we heard Father say:

"I am sorry, boys—the ladies have all retired." His tone suddenly grew very cordial as he continued:

"Why, Carlton! Loxley! Billy!—I didn't recognize you in this light. How are your families?"

At the mention of these names, we realized that the callers were our distant cousins, the Radford boys. We suddenly forgot our exhaustion. Mary started downstairs.

185

"It's the Radfords and I am going down," she decided.

Mary only got halfway down, for Father sensed that something was happening.

"Excuse me a minute," he said hurriedly and came into his room, which had a door near the stairway. My father thrust his head through this door.

"Get back up those stairs!" he shouted as loudly as a whisper will shout. "I told them you had re- tired. Now retire. Do you want to make me out a liar?"

By this time Caroline and I had joined Mary on the stairs.

"We've changed our minds," we chorused in whis- pers. "We want to see them."

Father saw that his night's rest was threatened. "Damn it," he said, "you haven't got any minds. Get back up those stairs!"

Mother now came tipping down the steps. "Mr. Yancey," she whispered, "the girls have changed their minds. They want to come down."

"Judas Iscariot!" My father could hardly control his whisper. "What in the hell is this—a whispering campaign? I won't let them change their minds. Let me handle this—you women will drive me crazy!"

Father left us gasping on the stairs, completely shushed by the violence of his whispers, and now he went graciously out to the porch, his voice exuding politeness:

"Boys, I am sorry! Indeed, I am more than sorry! I went to see if, by any chance, the ladies were awake. But they are all asleep. Please come again soon, and give my kindest regards to your parents."

After many expressions of regret had been passed back and forth, the Radfords were off.

My father burst into the house. He threw himself on his bed and began to groan aloud: "Damn women—nothing to do but change their minds— so many of them, and not but one of me——

"There I was—cement in my eyes—in my stocking feet, lying like hell to the children of my old friends—and *they* change their minds. It's a damned injustice that a man should be put in such a position. Damn!"

All of us still stood on the steps where Father had left us gasping. The whole episode had been so quick and tense, and now my father's outburst was so volcanic that we were suddenly overwhelmed with laughter.

"Well," my mother advised, "we had better go to bed and make an honest man of him."

We turned our steps upward and Mother, letting the others pass, fell in step beside me.

"You have spent rather a strenuous day appreciating your father," she remarked, continuing to laugh.

CHAPTER XV

Checks and Balances

᷍ ∿∿∿

OUR family represented three separate phases of Virginia life. Father was a distinct product of the old South. He was used to giving commands and he expected to have his commands obeyed without question. Still he had a strict sense of *noblesse oblige.* He believed, with the English, that justice should be swift and sure, but I have often known him to make great personal sacrifices in order to help the unfortunate families of criminals whom the duties of his office had obliged him to convict. Yet Father never used such self-conscious phrases as *noblesse oblige.* He would have scorned a designation so smug. He had an instinctive and even violent pride in himself: He was a man, and that dignified all mankind.

Above all things, Father took pleasure in the fact

that he was elected to his office by what are known as "the common people." But this did not mean that he considered any group of people "common." Once I, in describing a boy I had met, applied the term "common" and Father glared at me.

"What do you mean by 'common'?" he demanded. "Do you mean that the young man is a sneak and a liar and a bully? Or do you mean that he has had no advantages: that he uses bad grammar and wears poor clothes? I hope you are not presuming to judge a man's soul because of a rough exterior."

Another time one of my sisters was criticizing and analyzing an acquaintance of ours when Father haughtily interrupted, "Well, he's a man, I suppose. God made him!"

My mother never shot such sharp reprimands at anyone. She was the mid-Victorian Virginian. We Yanceys loved an argument, and the hotter it grew the more exhilarated we became. But Mother did not like to argue. She did not have a long succession of lawyers in her blood. When an argument got too hot for her, she would retire to a book, where things happened more to her liking and were not so noisy; and where she could disregard, without contention, whatever she did not care to accept.

No gentleman of my father's generation ever sat down and mapped out household expenses with his wife. His was but to raise the roof if the bills got too big. Figures meant nothing to my mother. She never knew how much money Father made. She did not know how much money it took to run the house. She just bought what she wanted and Father had to take it. He did not take it without protest, and Mother considered that Father's vociferous complaints more than made up for any extravagance she might commit. This sort of evened up the score between them. And this was the only way in which they balanced their budget.

All of us children were hard-crusted moderns. We didn't like any genealogy or talk about Virginia's past achievements imposed upon us. We liked to go places and do things, and we wanted everything that was considered stylish. We belonged to the age when Virginia was just beginning to become Americanized, and our main ambition was to reconstruct ourselves into our conception of little New Yorkers.

Because our grandfather and father had had professions after the War Between the States, we had started life with a good deal more than most of our friends. While Father's contemporaries were struggling along, trying to accumulate a comfortable living, Father himself was having a fair amount of ease. He had electricity put into his house in town while other people were still lighting their homes with gas, and he had two bathrooms installed when most of his friends considered one a luxury.

But Father had never been taught to deny himself anything. A good number of people around Lynchburg, from small beginnings and heroic economies, began to acquire rather sizable fortunes and, as we grew up, we gradually found ourselves with a good deal less than most of our friends. Father could never understand why this made any difference to us. From having been quite modern, compared to most of his generation, Father unexpectedly reversed his position. He began to maintain that the meager conveniences he had enjoyed in ante-bellum Virginia were good enough for us.

It was a great cause for complaint with us, for instance, that all of our friends had two tiled bathrooms. We had two bathrooms, of course, but neither of them was tiled, and our sense of inferiority on this score was hard to bear.

Whenever we mentioned the subject of tiles, my father simply snorted. He said he didn't care what in the hell he bathed in as long as he got clean. He had just as soon it would be a creek.

"Yes, but the So-and-So's have tiled bathrooms, and so have the Blanks and the Dashes."

My father said he didn't give a damn if they did. All the people we mentioned had bathed in tin tubs, in their bedrooms, until they grew up. A bathroom was for private purposes. It was not a show place. We would get no tiles out of him.

Sometimes Mother would put in her two cents' worth and say she thought tiles would be nice. And then my father would make the comment that Mother was a very beautiful woman, who had some lovely ideas about what money would do, but she didn't have a single damned idea about what money wouldn't do.

We did not get tiled bathrooms, and we had to manage to worry out our existence with that stigma upon us.

Father never failed to register audible protest when anything annoyed him, and this always seemed to keep one's relations with him foursquare. Life must have been a sore trial to him when his daughters began to have beaux, for nothing can exceed the trials of a man who has daughters with beaux. I should think his trials would be even greater than those of a man who has daughters with no beaux. At night, with the victrola going noisily and several couples dancing downstairs, or laughing and chattering on the porch, our house was seldom quiet. But Father did not take his trials lying down and that made us feel better justified in disturbing him.

My father frequently stayed up very late at night

himself; but when he wanted to go to bed early, he didn't want any noise going on. He didn't even want any lights on downstairs after he had gone to bed. We could often hear him stomping around in his room and then coming to the top of the stairs to see if his objections had had any effect. If you were just having a quiet tête-à-tête with your best beau you were never unaware if Father was upstairs. He could get into his bed and out again with enough force to shake the whole house. And he could throw his shoes on the floor with such violence that you expected the ceiling to fall upon your head. Then he had a great accomplishment in the way he snorted and sighed so loudly: downstairs, it sounded like a full-fledged steam engine which had just puffed into a railroad station.

My mother never made any retaliatory noises when we disturbed her at night. She would simply get a book and read until the house got quiet. Sometimes, after she had been kept awake especially late, she would come down to breakfast with her pretty eyes looking a little strained and weary. But she never said anything about the inconvenience we had caused her, and this always left one feeling guilty and selfish.

I suppose the real reason Mother became so interested in genealogy was because she found it hard to get any satisfaction out of her family in the present

THE VANISHING VIRGINIAN

age. She seemed to get great consolation out of the past, but whenever she said anything about ancestors my father would laugh. He told her she was taking advantage of dead people who couldn't defend themselves, and then my father would tease:

"You needn't look up any of my ancestors. I know all about them. You know, there used to be a large quantity of molasses exported from this country to Europe. My ancestors smuggled themselves over in the empty molasses barrels. That's how we all got here; and that's why we are all so sweet."

"You are the silliest goose that ever lived," said Mother, laughing in spite of herself. "But, just the same, you should be glad that I am compiling all of your fragmentary family history to be bound in one book. You should be proud to keep the record that your great-great-great-uncle, Robert Yancey of Tillotson Parish, was the first man in this country to preach the doctrine of universal salvation."

"Hah!" chortled my father, "he will never pay a single damned plumber's bill for me."

"And you should want your children to know," my mother went smoothly on, ignoring Father's comment, "that Charles Yancey, of Buckingham, made such important contributions to the early life of this state that Thomas Jefferson called him the 'wheel horse of democracy.' "

"I don't mind them knowing it," returned Father,

"as long as you make it perfectly plain that, if they are ever down and out, he cannot buy them so much as one fried-egg sandwich."

"And you should want your children to know that their kinsman, William Lowndes Yancey, was the most gifted orator of his time. If the South had won the war, he would have ranked as the Patrick Henry of the Confederacy."

Here my father laughed outright.

"The South didn't win," he remarked, "so I expect you will find that your encyclopedia only rates that gentleman as an agitator."

To tell the truth, Mother's hobby of genealogy occupied much the same place, in the eyes of her children, as did Father's hobby of the swimming pond. She claimed that she was doing all of this grinding work for us, but we knew she was doing it for her own diversion. There was a time, in the first enthusiasm of her studies, when Mother could not carry on an ordinary family conversation without dragging in someone who had been dead two hundred years or more. This was an awful habit, and none of Mother's children was any more in sympathy with her genealogical work than Father was. My sister Caroline said she was tired of hearing about the origin of all the roots and branches of our family. It was easy enough to pick out old Virginia families without any genealogy: They were the seediest-looking people in any gathering. All she wanted was plenty of pretty clothes. She wished Mother would spend less energy on genealogy and more on sewing.

About this time I read in a well-known magazine that "the rocking chair is a vulgar American innovation, invented by the homespun Benjamin Franklin. No sophisticated family," said this article, "ever has a rocking chair in the home." I took the thing very seriously. There were a lot of rocking chairs around our house and Mother liked to sit in them. Furthermore, as I have already indicated, she also liked to rock.

I could never bear to see Mother rock after I had read the rocking chair's condemnation in the well-known magazine. I began to nag Mother about scrapping all her rockers and, when I did, my mother would get that sweet, far-away look on her face. She didn't seem to hear what I said, but she continued to rock back and forth.

I laugh now when I think that I ever wished to belong to a "sophisticated family." I hope with all my heart, if there are any household furnishings in Heaven, that God has given my mother a rocking chair. It is a thorn in my flesh to remember how I used to pester her about her harmless indoor sport.

But Father was entirely different. We always knew exactly where we stood with him. He never sat with a sweet far-away look on his face. He made answer to us immediately in terms we could understand. And he was the same with the outside world.

My father had a very good friend who was numbered among the newly rich. I shall call his name Albert Woolford. After Prohibition came in, the old Piedmont Club, like all gentlemen's clubs, lost an important source of income and it seemed about to go on the rocks. The older members of the club got together and decided that their best hope was to elect, as president, a rich man with a good business head, and one who had a reputation for generosity. They all agreed upon Mr. Woolford.

When Mr. Woolford was informed of the honor which had been conferred upon him, he was very doubtful. He came to Father for advice.

"Bob," he said, "I know I can talk to you about what's on my mind. You know that I come from the plainest of plain families. I have been successful, but I do not claim to be anything but that. Now what would be your judgment of a man of my type accepting the presidency of the Piedmont Club?"

"Well, Albert," answered my father readily, "the matter of first importance is that every member of the club likes you. In the second place, the club needs a business head and it needs money. You have both. You are a rich man, but you are not the only rich man we could have selected. That, on the face of things is a compliment. I think you can accept with dignity."

When Mother heard what Father had told Mr. Woolford, she was very much concerned.

"I know you hurt the poor man's feelings," she said; "you should not have been so brutally frank. It's pathetic—he wants to be president of the club so terribly. You could have told him he had become such an important citizen that he was the logical choice. You could have told him *any*thing but what you did."

"Damn it, Rosebud," my father returned, "Woolford is an honest man. He asked an honest question and I gave him an honest answer. I wouldn't insult him with such evasions as you suggest. He appreciated it, too. He accepted today."

The Kall Building, where my father had his office, had been built by old Mr. W. P. Kall. Mr. Kall had come to Lynchburg soon after the War Between the States, and he had with him a few hundred dollars in gold coin. No gold money had been seen by any of our townspeople for years, and it was such a great curiosity that it was exhibited in glass fruit jars in the window of Mr. George Cooper's hardware store. With this gold coin Mr. Kall started a brokerage business. He grew quite wealthy, and after he had become an old man he married an extremely pretty young woman. Mrs. Kall attended her aged husband with every beautiful devotion, but of course she out-lived him, and after he had been dead for a time she took a successor who was poor but handsome and nearer her own age. So the new husband, Mr. Arnold, began to manage the Kall Building.

Father had always liked Mr. Arnold, and Mr. Arnold liked Father, I think. However, soon after the marriage took place, they had a little altercation. It was during that period after the World War when prices were soaring sky-high. Mr. Arnold came around to Father's office and told him he was raising the rent.

"I have been in this building ever since it was put up," said my father, "and I don't intend to pay any more rent than I have always paid. There's not a damned bit more space in this office now than there was when I came here."

"I am raising all the rents," explained Mr. Arnold. "I am not getting enough income from the money I have invested in this building."

"The hell you're not," answered Father. "You haven't got a damned cent invested in this building except the dollar you paid for a marriage license."

At this Mr. Arnold burst out laughing. He raised the rents of all the other offices, but he did not raise Father's. Besides that, he thought it was too good a story to keep. He told it to all of his friends and finally Mother heard it. Mother said it was dreadful of Father to have been so rude to Mr. Arnold. She said it was inexcusable of him to have reminded Mr. Arnold that his fortune came from his predecessor.

"You, who always claim to be for the underdog," continued my mother, "you should be the last person who would want to hurt Mr. Arnold's feelings."

"He wasn't hurt," Father laughed merrily. "He was a good sport about it. If he had been hurt he would not be spreading the story himself. For that matter, David Arnold has never been any underdog. He was no pauper. He was always a gentleman and he is still my friend. However, I am not always for the underdog. I am only for the underdog until he gets on top, for then he is sometimes insufferable."

My mother told Father that was a dangerous doctrine for him to preach. He should learn to control his tongue. He was too much like his ancestor, Alexander Leighton, the famous Scotch divine whose tongue Charles the First had ordered to be cut out.

My father replied that he had never heard of the fellow; so he couldn't have been particularly famous. But he did seem to remember that Charles the First had lost a more important appendage than his tongue.

CHAPTER XVI

Management or Mismanagement

∿∿∿

IT IS hard to form a clear and impersonal estimate of those who are very dear to us. I suppose my father was certainly a domineering person, but Mother was dominating. This was because she never wasted any energy blowing the top off the kettle. She went her calm, sweetly determined way in spite of all explosions.

Since Father was so fond of people he liked to go out in the evening and, as he thought Mother was highly ornamental, he always wanted her to go with him. But after Mother took up genealogy as an escape from the problems of a living family, she hardly ever would go. She usually had a headache from reading and making notes and pecking away at her typewriter all day.

Whenever Mother did go anywhere with Father

she was late getting ready. Of course, my father sometimes employed entirely unique methods of accomplishing punctuality; but punctual he was, to the point of military precision. The fact that Mother could never be on time for anything was a constant irritant to him. He said that, when it came to a consideration of time and money, my mother was the most maddening optimist he had ever seen. She thought time and money would do twice as much as other people expected of them.

When Father and Mother planned to go out to dinner or to the theater together, my father would be dressed and waiting a full hour before Mother got ready. He spent that hour walking up and down the library floor, registering every type of impatience. Once in a while he would make his way to the door of Mother's room and inquire:

"Great guns! Aren't you dressed yet? What are you doing now?"

"Why, Mr. Yancey, you *know* I told you I had a headache. I had to take an aspirin tablet and lie down a while before I could dress," Mother would answer sweetly.

"You live on aspirin! You're nothing but a drug fiend—can't you do a damned thing without a prop? What you ought to take is outdoor exercise instead of aspirin."

"Yes," Mother would say absently and quite imperturbably; probably she was sidetracking her mind from the importunities of her living husband to the more agreeable subject of ancestors whose faults, long ago, had been interred with their bones: "Yes —I'll be ready in a few minutes now."

The few minutes would stretch out indefinitely— with many exhortations from Father which did not exhort Mother at all. She never emerged from her room until Father had had time to snort off all his impatience. When she did appear she always looked so lovely and so absolutely innocent that Father forgot he had ever been irritated by her tardiness.

My father said that Mother never failed to enjoy herself immensely when she could be persuaded to go anywhere, but it was like blasting in a coal mine to get her started. And my mother said she really did have a nice time, but Father always stole the show from her in any gathering; talking was his profession and he always held the center of the stage.

Of course, my mother said, she was very proud to have a husband who was attractive enough to hold the center of the stage so successfully. "But," she added, turning her large clear eyes on Father, "I think it makes a much more pleasant evening if one person does not monopolize the conversation. I have always believed that listening and drawing other people out was a sure road to popularity."

"Bosh!" was my father's quick reaction to this. "Why should I exert myself to draw out a bore? If a person wants to talk, all he needs is two things: ideas and a vocabulary. Pretending to draw him out can't give him either. If he has both and doesn't like to talk, I consider it an absurd condescension to go through the motions of drawing him out. I am willing enough to listen to anyone who has something to say. But it is damned insincere to force conversation from a person whom nobody wants to listen to. There are many people who ought to be listeners. It is silly to encourage them to be anything else."

I suppose life is indeed much more satisfactory to a perfectly outright person such as Father was. I know my mother was constantly getting involved in things she couldn't do, simply because she never could answer a flat-footed "no" to any request. She was repeatedly being made president or secretary of something or other which she had no aptitude for running. As bills or letters to these various organizations came in she would merely stick them into some drawer, in whatever room she happened to be when they were brought to her. There the bills and letters would remain, sometimes unopened, and when the time arrived to take them up in a meeting, Mother never knew where they were. Quite often you would find them in your underclothes while you were dressing. And sometimes they were mixed up in the table linen, so that when you opened your napkin a bill or a check for a dollar dues would fall out. The fact that this happened to a certain gentleman who was a guest for dinner at our house one evening was a rather comical coincidence.

This gentleman, Mr. S——, was known to be a man of more than comfortable means, but he had the reputation of being, as the colored people say, "mighty tight-fingered with money." In fact, he did not pay his bills at all if he could possibly avoid it. He had many clever ways of avoiding it, and everybody knew about his eccentricity, so that his name was really a byword. Even I knew his reputation very well.

My father had run into Mr. S—— downtown and he had insisted that he come home to dinner with him. A Cumberland County client of Father's had sent him one of his famous old Virginia hams. No place in Virginia produces such hams as Cumberland County, said my father. He was having that ham for dinner and Mr. S—— must come home with him and have some of it.

It was not that Father had an overwhelming passion for Mr. S——. He had just happened to meet him as he was starting home. Anyone else would have done just as well. However, Mr. S—— was evidently in a mood for ham, so he came.

Being the eldest daughter at home at the time, I

was placed next to Mr. S—— at dinner. He was a very sociable sort of person and the meal was begun with a good deal of friendly chatter. As we finished our soup, however, Father's guest raised his napkin to his lips and, when he did so, a bill bearing the large letterhead of a well-known tinning and roofing establishment fell from the napkin and landed squarely in his lap.

I had seen the letterhead before. I knew it topped a bill which Mother had received for the repair of the roof of our church, and which the woman's auxiliary had agreed to pay. But Mr. S—— looked so violently startled that I could not help noticing his confusion. He shot a furtive glance at my father and quickly slipped the bill into his pocket. Besides that, his manner, all of a sudden, became rather strained. Though he had enjoyed his soup with keen appetite, his zest for the good old Cumberland County ham was not what it might have been.

My father saw that Mr. S—— was not having an hilarious time. He began to exert himself mightily. He turned on all his charm, and even his own family was hypnotized by his magnetism. But the third round of wine came on before Mr. S—— warmed up any.

Even so, Mr. S—— did not forget the billet he had hidden away. As we rose from the table he lingered a little, on the pretext of draining the last drop of wine from his glass, and I saw that he had a very apprehensive expression on his face: He was stealthily unfolding Mother's bill. A split second later, Mr. S—— slid Mother's roofing bill onto the dinner table and he turned to join the procession moving toward the library. He looked very sheepish. It was only when I saw this sheepish look that I understood the consternation Mr. S—— had shown when Mother's bill had fallen from his napkin. He had thought that my father, as a lawyer, was taking this delicate means of collecting a debt which, evidently, he had been trying to evade for some time.

When I told Father about his guest's strange behavior, he was vastly amused.

"By Jove!" he exclaimed. "So that's what was the matter with Anthony! I thought he had found a roach in the bottom of his soup plate!" Then Father broke into whole-hearted laughter.

"You know, this is the only time I ever got any pleasure out of your mother's unsystematic habits," he said.

Besides losing track of the business correspondence for her various organizations, Mother could never keep up with her purse. It was always misplaced; and when the vegetable man and the iceman and the milkman came around to collect their money, she did not know where she had put it. She would stand in the back hall, engaging such a tradesman in pleasant conversation about this or that, and she would say to any child or servant who happened to be near:

"Will you please look around the house and see if you can find my purse? Look in my top bureau drawer and, if it is not there, look in my secretary. It might be somewhere in Mr. Yancey's room. I had it up there yesterday."

Then would begin a long trek for anyone thus pressed into service. You would first search in all the places mentioned. Then you would look in all the chests of drawers and desks in everybody's rooms. Then you would examine the top of all the rows of books in all the bookcases, concentrating on the sections where genealogical and historical books were kept. Next you would feel inside all the large vases, behind the clocks and on top of the china cupboards. After that, you looked under the sofa pillows; you would poke into the table linen—into anything that might afford a lurking place for Mother's truant pocketbook. But it was indeed a miracle if you found it.

If you came back without it, Mother was not disturbed in the least. She would just make her naturally broad a's a little broader and say very graciously:

"I am sorry, Mr. Bibb, but I cyarn't find my purse anywhere. Would it be too inconvenient for you to come back tomorrow around harlf-parst two o'clock?"

I don't know exactly what effect the slightly broader a's were supposed to have upon Mr. Bibb or the milkman or the iceman. However, it never seemed to be too inconvenient for them to come back tomorrow. And Mother always timed their return so that, if her pocketbook did not show up by the time they arrived, my father would be in the house. She would then go to Father as he sat relaxing with his pipe after lunch and, with a perfectly angelic expression on her face, she would ask him for the amount of the bill she had in hand.

"Suffering Savanarola!" Father would exclaim. "You always want more money! Didn't I give you your weekly check just two days ago?"

"Yes, you did, of course," Mother would answer, looking at him ever so sweetly. "But I have misplaced my purse and I really have to pay Mr. Bibb today. This is the second time he has been back for his money."

"Such mismanagement—" Father would expostulate, getting out the money required; "making hard-working people waste their valuable time simply because you are too incompetent to keep track of your pocketbook. It is an outrage!"

My father always felt a little guilty when he kicked up such a row about Mother's incompetence.

He loved for her to have anything she wanted, because he actually thought she was a chip off the moon. But, in his own room, he had a place for everything and everything was kept meticulously in its place. It was simply maddening to him when Mother could not find her pocketbook. And yet he did feel a little guilty, I know, for if any of us children happened to be present at one of these pocketbook scenes he would turn to us and say, with a sudden burst of sincerely warm admiration:

"Your mother is really a very beautiful and lovely woman—a very intellectual woman." Then his exasperation would get the better of him and he would add with vehemence:

"But I'll be damned if she is not the worst manager I *ever* saw!"

Mother would look wounded at this. She said my father had married her because he thought she was pretty. He had not asked her if she was a good manager. She thought it was very unreasonable of him to expect her to have so many talents.

However, Mother had talents of management that my father did not even suspect. When she "ran across" her pocketbook it never occurred to her to mention it to Father or to pay back the extra sum he had advanced her. It was simply his loss and her gain. It left her children wondering if she had not planned it all along.

CHAPTER XVII

Court Scenes

vvvvv

THE judges of the court at Lynchburg must have suffered many sore trials over a long period of time during the years when Father and his father were acting as Commonwealth's Attorney. My grandfather was known to be a forceful orator, well acquainted with the law, but he was absent-minded, he had no sense of humor when he himself was involved in a joke, and he had a violent temper besides. I can remember, when I was a child, how the older citizens of Lynchburg used to laugh about a famous murder case that Grandpa once tried.

The prisoner in this murder trial was a gentleman with the odd name of Mr. Thimble. It was a case of the eternal triangle, involving Mr. Thimble's wife, and the person who was killed had been Mr. Thimble's best friend, a man who had lent Thimble a large amount of money to assist him in his failing business. Of course, the defense was contending that the friend had merely lent Mr. Thimble money on account of his guilty affection for his wife, and that Mr. Thimble was justified in what he did.

But Grandpa pictured Mr. Thimble to the jury as an unreasonably jealous husband who, in his wrath, had not paused for just explanation. And the murdered friend he drew as one endowed with every noble quality.

Here was a man brutally cut off in his early manhood, said Grandpa. He had trusted this villain Thimble with almost his entire fortune to save his shaky business. He had come to Thimble's house often—yea, often at Thimble's invitation, for it was to Thimble's advantage to have him where he could get at his purse strings.

He was a handsome young man—and charming —it was small wonder that Thimble's wife should have been attracted to one of his warm and generous nature. But she was as pure as she was beautiful. Ah—what a crushing thing it was to this lovely flower of a woman and this faithful friend to realize they had fallen in love. They knew there was but one thing to do: He must go away forever.

"Ah—forever is a long time," said Grandpa, "and surely one who is giving up his heart's desire, to save dishonoring his friend, may be pardoned for kneeling on the floor at her feet, for showering her hand with kisses as well as tears!

"But now Mr. Thimble comes into the house. He sees the tender scene. In view of his professed love for his wife, and his indebtedness to his friend, he might well stay his hand for an explanation. But no —stealing past the door he sneaks up to his room. There he keeps a pistol.

"And now a last good-bye: The young man rises to his feet. He places in the hand of his dear one a locket which contains a miniature of his mother.

" 'Symbol of all that is good and pure,' he says, 'token of all that I hold most dear; keep this always, for my sake, and know that my prayers are with you.' Weeping and bewildered, the poor young wife stands holding the locket in her trembling hand. And then——

"Then down upon this tender, sacred good-bye comes the raging husband. Down upon his broken-hearted friend and upon his wife, so good and true. He who had not the courage to face his friend un-armed. He who had sneaked past the door like an animal stalking its prey. He who could not render trust to the friend who had trusted him. Down he swoops like a wolf upon innocent lambs." Here Grandpa got excited by his own oratory:

"Yea—and without warning—charging down the steps comes Mr. Pistol with a thimble in his hand."

The eyes of the jury and everyone in the courtroom had been bulging with excitement as Grandpa
reconstructed the scene leading up to the murder.
Grandpa had a hypnotic voice and, in his old-
fashioned style, he could build up quite a drama. He
had made his audience so tense that when, at the
climax, he brought Mr. Pistol charging down the
steps with a thimble in his hand, everybody was
thrown into convulsions of laughter. They laughed
and laughed. Grandpa was furious. He stamped his
feet and yelled out that they were all damned fools;
but this only made them laugh more. And the more
they laughed the more infuriated Grandpa became.
He roared and ranted.

The judge couldn't get order. Every time he
banged with his gavel, and bellowed out for order,
someone else would make a remark about the vicious
Mr. Pistol who went around assaulting defenseless
people with a thimble, and the whole room would
go into hysterics again. Finally court had to be ad-
journed for the day because nobody could do anything but laugh about Mr. Pistol and his murderous
weapon.

Besides the fact that he often got himself entangled in his own oratory my grandfather's absent-
mindedness frequently interfered with the normal
course of justice in the court at Lynchburg. One
morning he was hurriedly getting his papers to-

gether to try a case when he missed his spectacles. He sat down and wrote Grandma the following note:

"Dear Lucy,

I cannot find my spectacles. I must have left them at the house somewhere. Please find and send them to me as quickly as possible.

Your affectionate husband,
Tudor Yancey."

Then Grandpa called his office boy, a young colored man named Jim-Ned:

"Jim-Ned, take this note up to my wife. Hurry as fast as you can. Come straight up to the courthouse with the answer. I can't start trying my case until you get there."

Just at this moment, Grandpa found his spectacles parked on his forehead. He folded them up and put them into his pocket. Then in great haste, he added a postscript to Grandma's note:

"P. S. Never mind about the spectacles, I just found them on my forehead. W. T. Y."

He handed the note to Jim-Ned:

"Now, don't waste any time, boy. Don't stop on the way for anything. Meet me in the courtroom!"

Jim-Ned started off at a trot. Grandpa grabbed his papers and hastened up to the courthouse. When he arrived there, he still had the idea fixed in his mind that he could not begin trying his case until Jim-Ned returned. The court waited patiently for Jim-Ned.

After so long a time Jim-Ned appeared at the door of the courtroom. Grandpa called out to him impatiently:

"Make haste, boy! You walk as if you were dragging a ball and chain. Did you give that note to my wife? What did she say? Did she send me my spectacles?"

Jim-Ned shuffled bashfully down to the aisle toward Grandpa. In his hand he carried a short piece of rope.

"Naw Suh, Mr. Tudor, she didn' send no spectacles. Miss Lucy she jest bust out laughin' when she read dat note I took her. She say ef you done already found yo' spectacles why in de world did you send me up dar wit dat note? She tole me to bring you dis here little piece o' rope. She say you so forgitful she 'fraid you gwine lose your britches."

Everybody in the room broke into loud laughter at this. Grandpa did not fail to protest vehemently. And that wasted some more valuable time which belonged to the State.

My mother used to say people told so many absurd stories on Grandpa that she had never believed the one about the spectacles. She said Grandpa got so angry when people laughed at him that she believed half the stories on him were made up only to tease the old man, because he was so funny when he got into a temper. But after Grandma died my mother found this note herself, written on yellowed paper, in Grandpa's own handwriting. Grandma had always kept it because she thought it was such a good joke, and she had scribbled a little comment of her own in one corner, with the date added. (This was one of the few letters that Grandma had left after the Great Fire of 1907, and how it happened to escape Mother's one housecleaning orgy in Grandma's room, I do not know.)

There was one big difference between the way my grandfather and my father wasted time for the Commonwealth of Virginia: My father did not mind who laughed at him. And the longer he could keep people laughing at him the better he liked it.

Once my father had a case against a young man who had been selling worthless oil stock around Lynchburg. This was a handsome and very suave young rascal, and he had been using his good looks and his ingratiating manner as a means for swindling unsuspecting widows and other susceptible females. In trying this case, my father described the young culprit as the "fellow with the face that launched a thousand gyps." And when a peal of appreciative laughter greeted this description, he continued to compare the prisoner with Helen of Troy in the most ridiculous way. He carried the young man all through the Trojan war, using Homeric language, and the parallel, in some places, was so funny that even the prisoner himself was laughing with the utmost abandon. Things got so unruly that the judge had to call a halt. Then everyone took a good breath and Father started off again—until the judge stopped him once more.

The judge was always calling a halt on Father, and I do not doubt that he had good reason to do so. I surely know enough about Father to realize that there must have been times when he tried the patience of the judge to an absolute breaking point. The judge was a very businesslike man; he liked an atmosphere of calm dignity to prevail in his court, and he himself was not given to flights of ridiculous fancy. And Father was the opposite of all this.

The judge and Father were quite good friends outside the courtroom, but in the courtroom they rarely ever clicked off together. And as far as my father was concerned, at least, there were reasons behind this paradox which can not be explained by the mere traditional border warfare between judge and State's attorney.

In the first place, while in court the judge had a position of authority over Father. Father had learned to give orders exceedingly well. He had never learned to take any. And he never did learn. My father thought he knew as much about points of the law as anyone alive; and when the judge ruled out any of his evidence, or sustained an objection of which he did not approve, he stood on his hind legs and argued with the judge. And if the judge did not come around to his point of view he called him what he thought the occasion demanded. And then Father was fined for contempt of court. And when this happened my father would snort out:

"What are we here for anyway? To get at the facts and at justice; or are we here to maintain the dignity of this court? All right then—if I am guilty of contempt of court you are guilty of contempt of justice. Take the fine! It was worth it!"

A second reason for Father's refusal to bow completely to the authority of the judge was, I imagine, one which dated back to their youth. They had both been courting the same young lady at one time, and the judge had won his suit.

My father had always loved horses and when he was in Lynchburg he had kept a span of spirited bays at the livery stable. With these, hitched up to whatever happened to be the last word in stylish vehicles, my father used to take his favorite young lady riding in the afternoon. But lawyers have to keep rather irregular hours. Father did not always finish at his office in time to drive in the afternoon. So he had given the livery stable instructions that, if he did not himself require the horses by such and such a time, they were to be sent around to the home of Miss——. She would take the horses out for exercise. This was an unusual compliment for Father to pay any young lady. There were very few people whom he allowed to drive his fine horses.

Fancy my father's indignation then when one day, while he was sitting on the porch at Mother's home (only of course she had not then thought of becoming my mother)—fancy his indignation when he saw his last word in stylish vehicles go rolling up the street, his fine horses prancing proudly in their shining harness and, sitting in the driver's seat, holding his very own reins in masterly fashion, the judge! (Only he was not then a judge, of course.) Yes, the judge, with Father's favorite young lady beside him! That was the end of Father's courtship of the young lady. And I have always imagined it had much to do with Father's cantankerousness in the courtroom.

But there was still another reason why Father found it irksome to submit himself to the authority of the judge. They were cousins. They were those inescapable Virginia cousins. Their grandmothers had been sisters. They were both descendants of the French Huguenot, Gideon Macon, whose brass name plate adorns one of the pews at Bruton Parish Church in Williamsburg. It is hard to honor a prophet in one's own family, or to accept his word as law.

My father's grandmother had been known as

"pretty" Betty Macon. But her sister, the judge's grandmother, had been "witty" Peggy. There was a hint of superior mental equipment there! And as little as Father cared about heredity, he used to feel it when Mother, in her enthusiasm for the past, would twit him about the cleverness of the judge's grandmother. My father thought he had inherited a fair wit himself.

"Pooh!" he used to say, "the judge has the same kind of wit you will notice in the Sphinx."

Coincidence is a peculiar force. There is no doubt that it has altered the face of the earth. Much has been written about the laws of chance, but the more intangible and yet, somehow, more purposeful vagaries of coincidence do not seem to fall under that head. On coincidence alone is based my belief that God has prepared a miracle in this world for each and every one of us, if we have eyes to see it. And the ludicrous pranks which coincidence will often play have convinced me long ago that God most certainly has a sense of humor.

My father loved it when coincidence played a prank upon him. He took the prank to his bosom and naughtily used it for his own purposes—and not infrequently he overused it. I am sure there was one time when the judge of the court at Lynchburg must have thought he overused coincidence most outrageously.

It happened once that my father was trying a Negro man for murder, and this Negro had a very, very dark skin. Someone had upset an ink bottle on Father's desk and Father, being engrossed in making his argument before the jury, had happened to lay his handkerchief in the large pool of wet ink. My father was presenting his case in this wise:

This colored man, Silas, was known to be a bad character. He had been paying marked attention to a young girl of his race. The girl herself had seemed pleased with his attentions at first. But she belonged to a respectable family. Her father and mother had told her that she would have to give up her undesirable suitor. On the night that the girl was killed she had been in the house alone. She had locked the front door and she sat sewing in her room. Silas came to the house. He was furious at finding the door locked. Loudly he knocked upon the door.

Here Father paused in his exposition. The day was very hot, and Father reached for his handkerchief to wipe the perspiration from his face:

" 'You open dis door, Jane, and let me in,' " Father now rasped out, impersonating Silas. At this the jury began to laugh immoderately. Father had inked his face with his handkerchief and he was as black as Silas himself! But unconscious of this he continued, this time taking the character of the young Negro girl:

" 'Go 'way, Silas. I can't see you no mo,' my mamma and papa will whup me if I lets you in.' "

More laughter from the jury.

"Angrily Silas beat at the door." With these words, Father vigorously began to go through the motions of knocking in a door, keeping up threats in the voice of Silas all the time—but before the door broke down, the jury was laughing so loudly that Father stopped short.

"*Now,* what is the matter?" he asked, giving way to a puzzled laugh of his own.

When the cause of all the hilarity was explained, Father was as amused as anyone else.

But the judge was irritated. He called for a pause in activities and he ordered Father to go and wash his face. Of course, the judge was right. But something in his tone provoked the rebel in Father and he refused to go and wash: There was no law which required him to present his arguments with a white face, insisted Father, and in this case he preferred black. He did not want to take unfair advantage of the prisoner. Here everyone except the judge laughed again. The judge refused to let the trial go on until Father had washed his face and Father would not wash. They had it back and forth.

After quite a while one of the lawyers, who was Father's great friend, Mr. Randolph Harrison, came over to where my father stood and said: "Bob, please go and wash your face—or else we may be here until doomsday. I have got to finish this case and get back to my office."

Of course, this was just the kind of a cue that Father could take. He never failed to comply with a request where he would not take an order. He now laughed good-naturedly: "All right, Ran, I will do it for you. But if we don't all watch our steps, we will soon be required to wear long, curly wigs in this court. And I would hate that. It would make my head itch."

So Father went away and washed his face. But he couldn't resist a last insubordination:

When he returned to the courtroom he walked over and stood for a moment at attention, before the judge's bench: face up, with the air of a V. M. I. cadet awaiting inspection. Then he executed a snappy salute, clicked his heels together, turned, and went to his accustomed place. This caused another roar of laughter in the courtroom and it was some time yet before the trial could proceed.

I do not understand what strange dynamic power Father possessed that enabled him to carry all spectators with him in an inexcusable scene of this kind. But he did have some sort of ability which made people ride along on a wave of high tension. And after it was over you felt as exhausted as if you had been pulled through a clothes wringer, or as exhilarated as if you had just had a shot of laughing gas.

Perhaps one reason why Father got away with so much in the courtroom was on account of the fact that convicting a fellow human being is a grim business, and most people concerned welcomed the relief of a little comedy. And perhaps it was partly because of the more personal fact that Father had so many real friends who were willing to go the limit for him. And the way this worked in his favor can best be set forth by an incident which happened after Father had become quite an old man.

Father had a youngish friend named Billy Williams, who was a member of a family that had always been very near and dear to us. Billy Williams had suffered the misfortune of losing both his legs, but he had good artificial limbs and he could get about quite well with the aid of a cane. The only thing that bothered Billy at all was steps. It was extremely difficult for him to manage steps.

My father's office was on the fifth floor of the Kall Building, and there was only one elevator to accommodate the entire structure. One day, Billy Williams was sitting in Father's office discussing some business matters when there was a great hue and cry of fire. The elevator shaft was on fire! People ran madly down the halls, yelling, raising a great clamor. They made for the stairs in droves, pushing each other, calling out in terror.

My father, at this time, was frail with the infirmities of old age. Billy, in spite of the loss of his legs, was a broad-shouldered, strapping young man. Father knew he could not get Billy down five flights of stairs in all this tumult without help. But in the noisy mass of people surging past his office door, no one would stop and listen when he sought assistance. However, though Father looked as if a gust of wind might blow him away, he had not lost any of the marvelous power of his lungs. He stood at his office door and yelled loudly for someone to rescue Billy. He raised a mighty uproar and he damned everyone who rushed excitedly down the hall without pausing to understand the nature of his plea.

"Deaf and blind," he complained to Billy, "— blind and rushing like a herd of steers!"

The building was now filling with suffocating smoke. Billy begged my father to go and leave him. But Father would not do that. He continued to keep up a terrific din, until his importunities were noticed and help was brought for Billy.

Not long after this my father was trying a case in court and he got into one of his altercations with the judge. The judge fined Father for contempt of court and that was routine stuff. But this time Father maintained that he was right in making his point and he said he had absolutely no intention of paying the fine. Then the judge ordered Father to pay the fine or go to jail. And Father replied certainly he would go to jail. He would be glad to go to jail rather than pay an unjust fine.

The courtroom was breathless. Nothing like this had ever happened.before.

Quickly a young lawyer rose to his feet. It was Tom Williams, the younger brother of Billy. If the judge insisted upon sending old Captain Yancey to jail, said Tom, he would go to jail too. The judge did insist.

So they went off to jail together, Tom with my father. And after a while our cousin Harrison Jordan, who shared Father's law office, went to the jail and got them both out.

When my mother heard of this latest misdemeanor of Father's she really was shocked:

"Heavens above!" she exclaimed. "What will those two old men do next? They are both in their dotage!"

It was our cousin Harrison Jordan who told Mother about Father and Tom Williams being put in jail. He thought it was a tremendously entertaining story and he imagined Mother would be amused by it too. But Mother thought this, at last, was the limit and she told my father so. But Father only laughed.

And then my mother began to say she didn't blame the judge for being exasperated with Father.

All of the laws in this country were based on English law. All of the courts in this state were conducted along the dignified lines which the early colonists had brought over from England. My father, of all people, should admire dignity in a courtroom, said my mother.

But Mother couldn't impress Father by citing English traditions. He had the most versatile nationality in the world. He could turn French, Scotch, English or pure Welsh in the twinkling of an eye. Or he could become a combination of any two, three, or all four of these—sooner than you could say "scat." But if ever Mother thought she had caught him in a hole with any of this, my father could change to a hundred-per-cent American. However, Mother couldn't corner Father there either: When she was unwary enough to try he would scrap the whole bunch of them. He would say to hell with the whole damned lot of foreigners (and the term "foreigners" used thus by Father meant all hundred-per-cent Americans, as well as Europeans): he was a free Virginian, with full liberty to do as his own conscience directed.

By this time Mother would have no come-back at all. She could not keep up with Father's agile, adroit, and perfectly comical flimflams. She would have become so confused and diverted by his quick thrusts and his lightning changes of character that she would give up flashing the sword for dignity's sake. She would drop into a chair and almost laugh her head off.

"Your father certainly is something," she would say, wiping tears of laughter from her eyes, "—and after all these years I still haven't found out what he is."

CHAPTER XVIII

Hunting Scenes

wwm

WHENEVER I see or hear the words "Virginia Counties" the immediate picture which flashes through my mind is something on the order of the popular hunting prints—without the pink coats. Perhaps the reason for this is that my earliest recollection hinges upon such a picture.

I am sitting in Grandma's old green and gold coach in the carriage house near the barn. I am taking my doll for a ride by jogging myself up and down and pretending that the coach is traveling. And this is a large labor for me because my small bare feet will not touch the floor of the coach. On the seat opposite me sits "Daughter," who has not yet become "Millie." She is making my doll a lovely silk bonnet. She has a beautiful speckled feather from the breast of a guinea hen which she will use as the last touch to the bonnet. All around us is a dim cloud of unexplored territory. I feel that I am a very long way from home.

Suddenly the dim cloud around us is filled with the thunder of horses. Piercing whoops and yells burst through the curtains of space beyond the carriage house. Somewhere in my mind a vague memory stirs itself into thought: "It must be Indians!" Wide with alarm, my eyes seek Daughter's. She will know what to do.

Daughter's amber eyes are quick with excitement. From them I see that if it is indeed Indians, it isn't going to be an unpleasant experience. Throwing down her sewing and grabbing my hand, she hurries me out of the open door and across the barnyard. Her excitement is contagious. Wildly I rush with her to the pasture fence. There Daughter deposits herself and drags me up to a perch beside her.

"Fox hunt!" she says.

A deliciously mad cavalcade dashes across our meadow! Hounds are yelping deliriously. I can see the long exquisite muscles of the racing horses. Their nostrils quiver. On their bellies and flanks is frothy white foam. Oh, gallant, beautiful horses! Oh, headlong, carefree riders!

"Why are they running, Daughter?"

Daughter does not answer. Tensely she clutches my small body with one arm, while with the other

231

she braces herself against the fence post. For the jump is just ahead of the hunters. The high rail fence near the road. Cheering, whooping, yelling, over they go, to the last man. The curtains of space close again.

And this was my first introduction to the fox-hunting Radfords and Nelsons. After that I grew well acquainted with the thundering hoofs, the yelping hounds and the ear-splitting whoops of hunters. At certain seasons, they plunged through our place without warning. They jumped most of the fences, but if the fences were too high they tore them down. And it was not unusual for them to ride down the crops.

My father never had a word to say against this trespassing. He considered hunting a gentleman's sport and he accepted the fact that some damage went along with it. I suppose also he was thinking of the trespasses that were forgiven him.

But our overseer did not see eye to eye with Father here. It infuriated him to be forced to take a week from his regular work to repair crops and fences, and to round up cattle and sheep that had strayed away. Once he got so tired of it all that he selected a strategic spot and put up a sign which read:

"No hounting aloud."

When my father came upon this sign he promptly took it down. He always kept the sign, however, because he said it was a classic in pure description and he enjoyed showing it to his friends.

We had no fox-hunters in our family. All of Father's dogs were bird dogs, but my brother Bob liked to go 'possum hunting. This was on account of the fact that, after he got his first job, his vacations were few but he could ride out to the farm and hunt at night.

Bob spent all his spare money on hounds and the place was overrun with them. He was never content with the kind of hounds he had. He was continually trading them for what he thought were better hounds. Certainly Bob's dissatisfaction with his dogs was perfectly natural, for it was a long time before he ever caught a 'possum. Finally Bob said there was one perfect hound he knew he could get if he only had the money. But nobody offered to help him out with the price of the one superlative hound.

Then Bob saved and saved. He would not even have his clothes pressed. Sometimes Mother felt so disgraced by his appearance that she would send his clothes to the cleaners and pay for them herself. Seeing her weakness, Bob found other ways of working on Mother; and at last he brought home The Hound.

233

We were all deeply disappointed. The Hound was a stupid-looking beast. He had red eyes, and he would lie around all day in a state of coma.

"Bob," said my mother, "I believe you were cheated in that hound. He doesn't look intelligent to me."

"Oh, yes he is, Mother. I have hunted with him. He is sleepy all day but he is a night-dog. You just ought to see that dog at night. He is like a keg of T. N. T."

On the very first night that Bob stayed in town and did not take his new hound out for exercise we found that he was, indeed, like a keg of T. N. T. He carried on like a caged tiger and nobody could sleep at all.

But at that the hound was not half so much like T. N. T. as Father was. He said he'd be damned if he wouldn't let the infernal beast out to roam around in the woods. He started down to the pen in his pyjamas.

But Mother heard him going. She gathered up a wrapper and did a rare bit of hurrying for her. She overtook my father before he reached the pen.

"Don't let the dog out," she begged. "He is not used to his new home. He will run away and never come back."

"I hope to hell he does," said Father.

"No you don't. It would break Bob's heart. The

boy has made great sacrifices in order to get this special dog."

"Oh well—damn!" said Father, in absolute exasperation. "You always have your way."

He went back to his room. For the balance of the night he and the dog kept up a lively competition.

Nobody thought of trying to sleep. My mother lit her lamp. She got out Chesterton's *George Bernard Shaw* and proceeded to entertain herself with "light reading."

My father worked out a performance all his own. With one of his steam-engine sighs he would periodically rise from his bed and stomp to his bedroom door. From there he would roar out curses at the hound. Then he would slam the door with the violence of a tornado, stomp back across his room and throw himself noisily back into bed. Here he would lie for a short while, groaning and complaining in tones which he pretended to muffle, but which were loud enough to be heard all over the house. After a few minutes of this he would jump up again and bang down all his windows. Then he would fling himself on the bed once more. But in no time at all he would be out of his bed and furiously slamming his windows up again.

"Damn it—I'll smother!" stormed my father. He started his routine all over. He kept it up until daybreak. At that time the hound became quiet and everyone snatched a few winks of sleep before break-fast.

Bob's new hound really did catch a 'possum, though. It happened rather soon after his arrival and it was a great triumph for us all. I don't know why. We certainly did not want a 'possum. But we had endured so much from the hound that we all felt proud when he came through.

The next logical move was for Bob to turn the 'possum loose, and for us to have the fun of watching it run to freedom in the woods while the hounds yelped excitedly in their pens.

Bob, however, had other plans. Like many people who have at last attained a long-coveted object, he became very possessive. He was going to possess his 'possum to the very fullest extent. He was going to eat it.

Nobody approved of this. Aunt Nancy edged herself into the conversation: The 'possum was too skinny, she said.

"Give him to me. I kin fatten him up," said Aunt Nancy.

"I can't give him to you. I am going to eat him myself," Bob answered decisively.

"Hoomph, white folks don't eat 'possums," Aunt Nancy argued scornfully.

"I am going to eat this one. And I will give everybody a piece," Bob announced, going generous.

" 'Possums lives in graveyards. Dey eats daid people." Aunt Nancy's voice took on a weird note, but she looked at Bob with keen eyes.

"Pooh! if you can stand that, I can."

Bob put the 'possum into a chicken coop all to itself, and he extracted a promise from me that I would feed the creature for him.

I hated to keep the little animal cooped up when I knew of Bob's ultimate intention. After all the sport it had afforded Bob, this seemed "a dismal thing to do." Every time I fed the 'possum I was tempted to let it out of the coop—just by accident. I felt as horrid and mean as the old witch in "Hänsel and Gretel" when I went out with the daily rations. I imagine it was family loyalty which restrained my impulse to free the little creature: for, of course, Bob was my brother, and this 'possum was not actually a relative. And, all during the fattening process, Aunt Nancy was evidently nursing a secret hope that Bob would finally abandon his design and turn the 'possum over to her. She took great pains to see that I fed it properly.

On the day that the 'possum was pronounced fat enough to eat, Aunt Nancy complained bitterly all the time she was preparing it for the table. She never had heard of no 'possum being put on no white folks' table. This was just the kind of 'possum she and Jake liked to eat—so young and fat and tender!

237

Nevertheless, Aunt Nancy cooked it up in her best style—head and all—and with a sweet potato in its mouth.

Then came the presentation! We are all seated at the table. Aunt Nancy comes in with the air of a great artist exhibiting her masterpiece and, with much ceremony, she places in front of my father the platter whereon lies the body of the little fat 'possum. It looks, somehow, like a small roasted baby, and the sweet potato in its straining jaws seems grotesque beyond words. A sick twinge passes over all our faces.

Now 'possum meat is very white and innocent-looking. It is positively corpse-like. When Father carved into the white, delicate flesh he turned as green as if he were crossing the English Channel on a rough day. But Father did his best to save the situation for Bob.

"Have some of Bob's treat, Mary?" he inquired, forcing an inviting smile.

"No, thank you," answered Mary quickly, with a horrified expression on her face.

"You will have some, won't you, Caroline?" my father asked hopefully, passing Mary an empty plate.

"No, thank you, I believe not," Caroline giggled.

"Will you have some, Beck? 'Possum is considered a great delicacy," urged Father.

But I would not be persuaded. I was having a

desperate struggle simply to remain at the table.

Father did not take any either. And it goes without saying that Mother did not. My mother would never eat even a chicken with whom she happened to have a personal acquaintance.

Nobody took any 'possum except Bob. Bob tried to stick to his guns. But, after he had been served, he took one bite of 'possum meat and then he hastily covered up what remained on his plate with two large slices of broiled tomato.

So, after all, Aunt Nancy did get most of the 'possum.

Father, of course, never went 'possum hunting. He hunted only for birds, though he usually brought in a few rabbits. Father was an excellent shot and even after all these years young enthusiasts of the sport still love to tell tales about his exploits. They say he used to make a bet that he would bring down two birds with every shot. It was easy to get odds on a bet like that. But the trick in it was, they say, that "Old Cap'n Bob" would not shoot until two birds crossed each other in the air. Then he would pot them as quick as lightning; and he always won his bet.

I have never known what to believe and so I do not know if this tale is true. However, I do know that in the fall my father would come home laden with partridges and woodcock and sometimes pheasants and wild turkeys. But we hardly knew the taste of any of them. This was not because Father was lacking in generosity to his family; quite the contrary: He had seven children who were always ahead of him in the matter of hospitality. It sorely tried his genial soul not to be able to entertain his own friends as often as he wished. So, when he had enjoyed a successful hunt, all of the choice game was for his own particular friends. He gave us the rabbits.

My mother did not like Father's game suppers in the least. She had to stay in the kitchen all day long superintending the cooking of the particular delicacies that my father liked to have for his particular friends. Anything so delectable as pheasants and partridges and wild turkey had to be cooked just right. It would have been a sacrilege to risk having them ruined. So into the kitchen my mother would go.

Mother would have to be in the kitchen all day because, aside from the actual game for my father's suppers, all sorts of complicated old Virginia recipes had to be interpreted. Even granted that one's cook could read, she would not know what a "gallipot" was. She would not know, when a recipe required a certain amount of isinglass, how much gelatin was the modern equivalent of that. Nor could she understand that, for a certain portion of cream of tartar and soda, one could substitute an exact amount of baking power. But Mother had the old-fashioned instinct for really perfect food. There were some things which turned out right only if my mother made them herself.

If ever you go to Washington's birthplace at Wakefield, or to Williamsburg, and some attendant hands you a pamphlet of old Virginia recipes requiring dozens of eggs, quarts of rich cream and all kinds of rare spices and herbs, do not imagine for one instant that present-day Virginians live upon such sumptuous fare. Those dishes, like the courtly manners one reads about, are not for family use. They are for "company."

We never got any of the Olympian food that was prepared for Father's suppers. The next day we sometimes had a little turkey hash. But it was very weak. We always contented ourselves with rabbits, knowing full well that was all we could get.

All unexpectedly, one fall, our rabbits turned into a great sensation. My mother had been visiting in Amherst and an old English lady had given her a recipe for "jugged hare." My mother was delighted! At last she could have something very special out of the numerous, tasteless rabbits which fell! to our lot during hunting season.

The jugged hare was a huge success. You cut the rabbit into pieces about the size of fried chicken and you added diced carrots and strips of bacon and whatnot. The whole mixture, with enough water added to cover it, was put into an earthen pot and cooked all day in a slow oven. It was delicious.

My father scorned rabbits and for a long time he could not be prevailed upon to touch the jugged hare. When at last he did try it, jugged hare became the prize dish at his game suppers.

After that we never got any more rabbits.

CHAPTER XIX

Black and White Again

wwv

ANY man who has such an exaggerated personality as Father had, generally makes many enemies.
One hardly ever hears anything about the enemies
a member of one's family makes. This fact is a monument to the fundamental kindness of the human
race. On the other hand, a fairly good index to the
number of enemies a man has, is the number of people he himself dislikes. Father was an extremely
outspoken person. He never left anyone in doubt as
to how he felt on any subject, and yet I cannot recall
more than four people of whom he ever expressed
disapproval.

The first was a man who was widely respected
as a public-spirited citizen. He always identified himself with movements for "civic betterment," and
everyone took him at face value. But Father said

this man was as crooked as a barrel of fish hooks. He never went near him if he could help it.

The second man my father described as a perfect ass. He admitted that he really had nothing against the fellow, except that he was eaten up with self-importance. Father said that when this man walked down the street he looked like a whole procession coming: It wasn't very pleasant to be with anyone so pompous as Bernard Parr; so he made it his business to avoid him.

There were two other acquaintances of Father's whom he described as "lax in their morals." This could have been overlooked except for the fact that they each, in a very conspicuous way, used the church as a cloak to cover up their irregularities. Father thought these two men polluted the very air he breathed. He looked positively ill if he had to be anywhere around them.

Why our young friends did not hate Father I have never been able to understand. As I have said, he was often rude to them. And he was rude to them more often when we were staying in the country than when we were in town, for there was the eternal problem of transportation.

Father came up on the train, of course, and no one needed special permission from Father to ride on the same train with him. But our house was three miles from the station. Any young man who wanted a date with one of us would have to call Father's office during the day to make sure that Father was in town; that Father was going out that evening; that there would be an extra seat in the automobile from the station; that there would be room for him to spend the night; and, more important still, that he could get back to his job in due time the next morning.

When Father was put through this questionnaire, as likely as not he would roar out that he was busy as hell. He did not have time to hang on the telephone all day arranging engagements for a lot of brainless young puppies. "The train leaves at half-past five, and you've got two good feet. Do as you damn please." As likely as not, he would bang up the telephone with something like that.

Nevertheless, at the end of the day, Father would arrive at Forest Depot, smiling, and on the most intimate terms with the very person whom he had treated to such a show of impatience in the morning. And, as likely as not, they would be laughing at the very insults that Father had indulged in at his guest's expense.

Sometimes I used to ask my mother why young men never failed to like Father, in spite of his rudeness to them. If Mother happened to be annoyed at Father at the moment she would say:

"They understand him because he is just an adolescent himself."

But if my mother was not vexed at Father she would answer:

"Well, look at him yourself—at his age, still doing the things young people like. Nobody enjoys the thought of getting old. Maybe he is a guaranty to them that they can overcome old age."

"I still don't think that explains why he can insult people and get away with it. They think it's funny when he does it. They like him. They even admire him!"

My Mother would laugh at this:

"They admire him because he behaves just exactly as everyone would like to behave. Most people are afraid to be natural for fear of appearing ridiculous, or of being unpopular."

"Well, *I* don't admire *that* in him. He embarrasses me beyond words."

"Of course he embarrasses me too," my mother would reply. "But I don't mind being embarrassed nearly so much as I used to. As I grow older, the chief thing I have to fight is boredom. Even when your father embarrasses me most I find him diverting. You are never bored when you are embarrassed to death."

I did not like any of Mother's explanations. I

made up my mind that Father was just a cross I would have to bear.

It used to make me squirm when Father would quiz every boy that ever came to see me: Who his father was, what was his profession; who his grandfather was, what was his profession. At one time, I had a very particular friend named Edmund Drake, who happened to be from Oklahoma, and who was at college in Virginia. My father had never been in the Middle West in his life. He did not know anyone in Oklahoma except Senator Owen, who was a migrated Virginian. Oklahoma being a state as large as many European countries, I knew perfectly well that a person from Oklahoma might be very nice indeed and still not know Father's friend, Senator Robert Owen. Therefore I suffered great mental discomfort when Father asked Edmund if his family knew the family of Senator Owen. No, was Edmund's reply; of course he knew that Owen was the Senator from Oklahoma who, with Carter Glass and Samuel Untermyer, had worked up the Federal Reserve laws; but his family had no personal acquaintance with the family of Senator Owen.

On receiving this negative answer, Father immediately subjected my friend to a drastic third degree. He wound this up by asking Edmund if his family owned their home!

"No," Edmund answered; "you see, I am an only child. My mother has always preferred to live in an apartment, because it gives her more freedom."

"That surprises me," remarked my father. "You know down here we don't think a man amounts to anything unless he owns his home."

I was aghast at this comment. I knew that Edmund's family could buy our two modest establishments just for the fun of burning them up, and never feel the strain. I knew his mother traveled around the world whenever she pleased; spent the winters in Florida; and went to New York for the opera as casually as we would run down to Lynchburg to a movie.

If I had not been so young I suppose I could have enjoyed Father's typical Virginia attitude on the subject of owning one's own home, and of having some sort of tangible roots in the soil upon which one lives. But I could only boil with inward rage at that time. And I later apologized to Edmund for Father's third degree.

Edmund was surprised at my apology. He said he did not get any impression of a third degree. He felt that Father was merely interested in comparing notes on different sections of the country.

"You know, your father is a grand old gentleman," he added; "I like him."

My mother was certainly much nicer to Edmund

248

than Father was. But, from the first, Edmund seemed irresistibly drawn to Father.

And it was not only Edmund. Any young men who came to see one of Father's daughters would forget the object of their visit and follow Father around, just as chickens follow a mamma hen, if they could find the flimsiest excuse for doing so. He would ask them the most personal questions. He would be nasty to them when he chose. When he got tired of them he would scat them away exactly as he used to disperse us when we were babies listening to his story-telling. But later, if they saw even so much as an encouraging twinkle in his eye, they were at his heels again. It was something nobody could explain. It was quite disconcerting to a young lady who was trying to make a definite impression upon an indefinite young man.

Another person whose deep attachment to Father never made sense was Aunt Nancy. He would swear at her on the slightest provocation: if his breakfast was half a minute late; if he sent her on an errand and she did not get back in an impossibly short time; if he wanted Uncle Jake and she could not find him immediately. Any such trifle would cause him to roar at her the undeserved accusation that she was as slow as cold molasses; that she didn't give a damn if she *never* carried out his instructions; that she was so stupid she must have hook worm.

I don't think there was ever any danger of Father's throwing things at Aunt Nancy. But sometimes he yelled at her so loud it seemed that he might burst to pieces in her face.

And all of his accusations were untrue. Aunt Nancy was as wiry and quick and alert as a human being could be. She would have been justified in violently resenting Father's false condemnations. She would have been justified if she had sulked all day. But she never did either. She would go up to the kitchen and nearly split her sides laughing. And after the most severe lampoonings from Father, I have seen her drop down on the kitchen steps and rock back and forth with tears of uncontrolled mirth streaming down her face.

Our beloved Uncle Jake died during the last summer I ever spent at Forest. He must have been nearly a hundred years old. We had never known him to be really ill. But one morning he did not wake up; and when Aunt Nancy came and told us about it we could not believe that he was gone.

This was the first time I ever saw my father so overwhelmed with grief that he was quiet and meek. He did not go to his office, and all day he roamed around the farm, silent and disconsolate. On the day of Uncle Jake's funeral he was like a lost child. We all went to the little wooden church which was near our place. We sat together at the back so as not to interfere with the seating of the colored congregation. We were dimly worried about Father—sorrowful at parting with our old friend.

The preacher at the little country church was a handsome mulatto who rejoiced in the high-sounding name of Jefferson Monroe. When he arose to begin the service and saw us sitting grief-stricken in the back pew, he announced that his salary had not been paid for three months, and he fixed my father with a piercing eye. He said he would not go on with the funeral until his back salary was paid.

I, for one, was shocked that Jefferson Monroe should take this occasion to mention such a thing as money. I looked for Father to spring to his feet and tell him exactly what he thought of him. I looked for Father to tell Jefferson Monroe to go to hell—that he would perform the burial himself. But Father did not utter a word of protest: With profound, and perfectly detached dignity, he went forward and laid in Jefferson Monroe's hand the sum he had demanded.

My mother used to say that Uncle Jake was many years older than Aunt Nancy. But after Uncle Jake's death Aunt Nancy slowed up a good deal. My father was deeply concerned about her health, and finally he told Aunt Nancy that something must be wrong. She would have to go to Lynchburg and get

herself examined. This frightened Aunt Nancy almost frantic. She did not want to get herself examined but just the same she went, for Father's
word was law with her.

The doctors in Lynchburg found that Aunt
Nancy had a tumor. At her age, they hated to risk
removing it but, on the other hand, they could not
risk leaving it in. Aunt Nancy did not want an op-
eration. The very thought of it scared her stiff. But
Father told her she must have it, and so she did.

Aunt Nancy had two sons and a daughter who
lived in New York and they were quite well off. My
father had a large and expensive family. When I
think of all the evening shoes and tennis rackets and
silk stockings he was expected to buy, I don't see
how a mere lawyer ever did it. It seems to me that
a man would need to be at least an automobile man-
ufacturer in order to do all that was expected of
Father. Slavery times being past and gone some fifty-
odd years, anyone would think that Aunt Nancy's
sons and daughter would naturally have assumed her
hospital bills. But the question never came up. Such
a question never occurred to Father.

It was a great sight to see Aunt Nancy in the
hospital. Her sons and daughter came down from
New York in a large shining automobile and they
brought her more finery than she had ever had in
her life. We would come to Lynchburg in our very

unpretentious car which, in the summer, was gen-
erously splashed with the red mud of Bedford County,
and we would bring Aunt Nancy such homely of-
ferings as a bouquet of garden flowers, or a few
ramekins of baked custard. And, when we arrived
at the hospital, we would find Aunt Nancy's room
resplendent with hothouse flowers and baskets of
gorgeous fruits. She herself would be adorned in a
brilliant pink silk bed-jacket, queening it over her
assembled family who were encamped around her
bed, basking in the importance of her position as
an invalid.

We had never seen Aunt Nancy in anything but
the cleanest and neatest black-and-white printed
calico. It was unbelievable to see her so transformed.
But there she lay, propped upon fancy pillows,
dressed like the queen of Sheba, and evidently enjoying herself hugely.

We thought the days of the years of Aunt Nancy's
usefulness to us were over. We thought that, having
had a taste of such luxury and importance, her head
would be completely turned, and Caroline and I
were discussing these probabilities when we went
down to Lynchburg to bring her back from the hospital.

But, when we opened the door of her room, we
found Aunt Nancy dressed in her neat black-and-
white calico. She was stepping around right briskly,

253

cleaning out bureau drawers and folding up all of the glad rags that her family had brought her. When she had wrapped them up in a tidy paper package she handed them to her daughter and remarked with elaborate casualness:

"Here, Harriet, take these back to New Yawk with you and use 'em for your next show."

Aunt Nancy was so pleased with herself over this sally that she lost no time in telling Father about it after we had picked him up at his office.

"Nancy," said my father, "I always knew you were a black devil, but I never knew before that you were a black cat."

They both laughed with immeasurable delight.

After Aunt Nancy's return to Forest she immediately snapped back into her regular routine. I paid very little attention to her because I was busy with the absorbing process of getting myself engaged.

Almost every country place in Virginia has some sort of lovers' lane. Besides its really important uses, a lovers' lane adds to the pastoral beauty of a country place. But our lovers' lane was not a lane at all. It was actually more suggestive of Druids and human sacrifice than of things pastoral. It was a large semicircular clearing surrounded by gigantic oak trees, and in the very center of the clearing was an immense boulder. But whoever had designed this lovers' lane had overlooked the factor of privacy; for one side of it was open to inspection from the county road.

The colored people in the country have their church services in the afternoon. However, such things as colored church services can easily be overlooked by one who is occupied with the absorbing process of getting engaged. . . .

One Sunday evening I happened on to a chair on the porch; and the chair happened to be near the dining-room door. I was wondering how I could conceal a certain ring until a propitious time should arrive for making its acceptance known.

In large families things are always being overheard. In our large family someone was usually talking in each room in the house and, if you happened to be near, you heard what they were saying. In our family, if people had secrets to impart, they went off together and shut doors and spoke in whispers; or they took a walk. Anything else was considered general information. None of us would have dreamed of listening at keyholes but, at home, I never felt that I should cough, blow my nose, stamp my feet or burst into sudden song if ever I overheard my name mentioned in a casual conversation.

On this Sunday when I dropped into a chair on the porch, pondering the problem of my newly acquired ring, I heard Aunt Nancy come into the dining room and begin setting the table for supper. My mother entered soon, and she gave Aunt Nancy some instructions about extra places for the meal. The next thing I became aware of was Aunt Nancy saying:

"Miss Rose, I know Miss Rebecca is goin' to marry dat Mr. John."

"Why?" asked my mother in a voice entirely devoid of curiosity.

"I know she is, dat's why. When I come from church today, dar she was up dar in dat clearin' in de oaks. She was a-settin' on dat big rock; and Mr. John was settin' on de ground at her feet lookin' up at her like she was Jesus."

"Aunt Nancy!" my mother expostulated in a shocked voice. "You should not make such comparisons. That is blasphemy."

"Maybe so," replied Aunt Nancy, undaunted, "but anyway, I know she is goin' to marry him 'cause she was lookin' at *him* like he was Gawd."

Here my father came into the dining room and Aunt Nancy made her announcement to him. Then she went sailing up to the kitchen, leaving my mother now aroused, and pouring her objections into Father's ears:

She did not like John's profession. He was not intellectual. He was not handsome. Why couldn't I make up my mind to marry my cousin, James Hamilton, who was assistant editor of the —— *Times?*

He was both intellectual and handsome. He was everything she had always wanted in a son-in-law. He had such an aristocratic nose. Father should interpose before it was too late to break up this affair with John.

"Oh damnation!" exclaimed my father. "Is the child choosing a husband or are you choosing a son-in-law? Why do you want your daughter to marry a nose? You are making an airplane out of a mosquito! The nose is not important. Character comes first. Can the child be happy with this young man? Can he support her? To hell with the other objections."

And so my mother's objections were overruled. I married John and we came to Richmond to live.

CHAPTER XX

The Old Guard Does Not Surrender

∿∿∿

MY FATHER had always had many reasons for coming to Richmond. Sometimes he came to confer with the Governor about pardoning criminals. Sometimes he had to argue cases before the Court of Appeals. Sometimes—in fact, every two years—my father came to Richmond when the General Assembly was in session. This was in response to requests from friends that he advocate the passage of bills in which they happened to be interested. However, during legislative sessions, Father came more often to oppose bills which he himself considered damned foolishness and bad for the people. There were times when Father came to Richmond to make speeches of presentation at the unveiling of statues or portraits; and he came to introduce people who were making speeches of presentation. And then, rather often, my father simply came down to go hunting with some of his friends, using Richmond as his headquarters. But whatever brought Father to Richmond he would not stay with us. Regardless of all I could do, he would go to the Westmoreland Club.

"I don't like these suburbs of Richmond," he would say, although we ourselves felt that our house was rather central; "I feel strange in them. And besides, very few of my old friends are still living. If I don't stay at the Westmoreland I may never see them again. I can visit you after they are all dead and gone."

It never seemed to occur to Father that he might die himself before he ever paid us a visit. With this thought in mind, I allowed myself to become quite upset when Father, for the sixth time, permitted us to meet his train and then refused to be our guest. But my husband, as usual, took Father's part.

"Don't try to persuade him," John begged. "It isn't right. He would have a dull time with us and he loves it at the Westmoreland. You know people his age don't realize that Richmond extends beyond Monroe Park." All of this in an undertone as he attended to having Father's bags put into our car.

We started downtown for the Westmoreland. I talked about everything pleasant I could think of. I tried not to let my father see that I was hurt. But

I did not succeed. Suddenly, in the middle of what I was saying, he turned a penetrating glance on me and, interrupted my chatter:

"You do not like Richmond very well, do you, child?"

"I like Richmond well enough b-but I get homesick," I replied shakily, and looking up I saw that Father, too, was very close to tears. It seemed for a moment that Father might allow me to weep upon his shoulder. It even crossed my mind that he might renounce his cherished desire to stay downtown.

But just as suddenly as he had seen through my superficial chatter my father took himself in hand:

"Now look here, Beck, the easiest thing in the world is to be a martyr. You know how I hate to preach to people. I always assume that any intelligent person knows at least as much as I do. It irritates me when they don't. What you ought to do is to stop running up to Lynchburg so often.

"How long have you been married?" he shot at me.

"Four years."

"Four years!" exclaimed my father. "And you still get homesick! You are not showing much adaptability, are you? I think it is high time for you to face the fact that Richmond is your home.

"Now take a lesson from an oyster: An oyster is the dumbest creature on earth. It can't express itself even as well as a fishing worm. And yet even an oyster has the sense not to waste energy protesting and complaining. It gets to work and turns an inescapable irritant into the most beautiful of all jewels.

"You can be a homesick martyr if you prefer. That is one course you can take. The other course takes intelligence and adaptability. Now, have you got intelligence and adaptability, or have you not? And if not, where did *I* ever get a daughter without the brains of a damned oyster?"

I gulped at Father's lightning change of mood. It was like a glass of cold water dashed into my face. I mean glass and all. I did not pause to consider how poorly my father practiced the virtues of an oyster, but all at once I felt an overwhelming passion to try myself. At any rate, I saw that I could not use Father for a wailing wall. And Father went to the Westmoreland Club.

After this I applied myself to emulating the humble oyster and I did not venture to show my face in Lynchburg until the following Thanksgiving: How pleased Father would be that I was taking his advice. He would be sure to compliment me upon my cultivation of adaptability. But I did not catch Father in the mood for passing out compliments. He was busy with his own affairs and we only saw him on the run.

As we drove up to the back of the house in

Lynchburg Father was just emerging from the back door. He was dressed in his awful old hunting clothes and he looked like a tramp. But this never seemed to occur to him. He hailed us with cordial unconcern. He could only stop long enough to speak to us; he had just come out for his dog. He had to meet two friends at the train. He was due to catch the street car as soon as he could get Danny out of the garage. No, indeed—there was no use for John to take him to the train. The street car would put him there at exactly the right time. Lunch was just over. We must go in and have something to eat before it was too late.

We stood waiting for Father to get his dog and go before us up the steps.

The street car goes past our house in Lynchburg. About three blocks up the street there is a section of double track where the west-bound car has to wait for the car that goes downtown. So whenever anyone at our house wishes to catch a street car going downtown he has a perfect signal. He must start out for the corner when the west-bound car goes up the street. This will allow him only a comfortable amount of time before the downtown car arrives at our stop.

Thus we stood waiting for Father to pass, knowing that he must be on time at the corner in order to catch his car. Indeed, just at this moment, we heard the west-bound car moving slowly up the street.

My mother came to the back window and called in her gentle voice:

"Oh, Mr. Yancey, the car has gone up."

But Father was headed for trouble. His dog was chained to the rear axle of his automobile and who-ever had put him there had carelessly twined the chain through the spokes of the wheel.

At the sound of my mother's voice Father broke off his conversation with us. He undid the end of the chain which was fastened around the axle and with a quick jerk he started forward. If he had no-ticed that the leash was twisted through the spokes of the wheel he was far too excited to stop and dis-entangle it. Poor Danny's head went bang against the automobile wheel; his eyes bulged almost from their sockets and, of course, he couldn't follow Father.

My mother reappeared at the window.

"Mr. Yancey," her soft warning came again, "the car has gone up."

My father gave the chain another mighty pull— and another. It looked as if Danny's head would come off with the last one, and he let out some hor-rible half-strangled yelps.

My mother returned to the window.

"Oh, Mr. Yancey the car has gone up." The words

floated out with the liquid sweetness of Hawaiian music.

My father was finally down on his knees unwinding the chain from the wheel. His whole body was tense—charged with high voltage that seemed to electrify the atmosphere of the entire back yard. We stood watching, speechless, while his hands worked at the loops of the chain with inspired swiftness. He made no reply to Mother and she went away again. But in only a few seconds she was back at the window with the same gentle announcement:

"Mr. Yancey, your car has gone up."

At last my father had disentangled the chain. He leaped to his feet and, dragging the yelping Danny behind him, he bounded up the back steps, taking two at a time:

"Well," he fairly bellowed, "I am coming as fast as God will let me!"

My father rushed through the hall to the front door, where he had to stay his flight long enough to pick up his gun. He did not miss his car, because when the conductor saw him come tearing out of the house, shotgun in one hand and a now happily racing Danny straining at the leash in the other, he stopped the car and waited for Father.

* * * * *

My father had now reached an advanced age. He

had been Commonwealth's Attorney of Lynchburg for thirty-four years and my mother said that was long enough. She said my father should retire gracefully and not stand for reelection in 1929. But Father could not agree with Mother here. The truth is that he had been State's Attorney of Lynchburg for so long that he considered the office his own prerogative. It just wasn't in my father to give up his office.

As a matter of fact, this same disagreement had come up in 1925. My mother had insisted that Father ought to withdraw from local politics. He was well past seventy years of age. He ought to get out and content himself with a small law practice. This was what my mother had said to Father in 1925. But, of course, the reason behind it was that Mother had never imagined that Father would be reelected. She wanted him to retire in order to save him the blow of a defeat.

Nobody thought Father could be elected in 1925 because, in that year, the candidate who opposed him had the support of the Ku Klux Klan. And Father scorned the Ku Klux Klan with the most outspoken contempt.

"Anti-Jew, anti-Catholic, anti-Negro!" said my father scathingly. "Why don't they reduce it to a summary and conclusion and call it anti-Christ!"

My father could not fight the Ku Klux Klan hard

enough to suit himself. It was an insult to the South that the name Ku Klux had been revived. Historically, it had been necessary. The only purpose of its existence had been the protection of a defenseless people during a period of national madness. It had been disbanded by its own members as soon as the necessity for its existence was at an end. It was an insult to the memory of those first, desperate Klansmen that the name should now be made to stand for boycotting the rights of some of our best American citizens.

Whenever my mother would hear of the things that Father was broadcasting against the Ku Klux, she would shake her head. "If your father really wants to win this election," she would say, "he had better stop his bitter attacks upon the Ku Klux Klan. The temper of the working people has gradually been changing ever since the World War. The working classes are tired of paternalism in politics: the people of this new generation want things in their own hands. A good many of them take the Klan seriously. Your father shouldn't antagonize them in this way."

My father had a very devoted friend named Mr. Thomas Welch. He was a blacksmith—a great giant of an old man—and he and his father and grandfather had shod horses for people around Lynch-

burg for about a hundred years. During all of my
father's career in local politics Mr. Welch had been
his ear-to-the-ground. And Mr. Welch was tremendously disturbed about Father's lack of restraint in
his criticism of the Ku Klux Klan. He came to our
house one Saturday afternoon to warn my father
that his course was unwise.

"Cap'n Bob," he said, with genuine concern written all over his broad honest face, "Cap'n Bob, sir,
I know just exactly how you feel—but you can't
keep this up and be elected. 'Tain't like it was during Prohibition. The people is different now. The
gossip is that a man can't git nowhere in politics
without the Ku Klux backs him. I don't ask you not
to dislike 'em. I just ask you not to dislike 'em so
loud. If you keep a little quieter I think we can git
you elected."

"Ku Klux!" snorted my father unsubmissively.
"Ku Klux! Wolves in sheet clothing! Wolves snap-
ping at the throat of democracy," said my father in
a voice that made my backbone tingle, even though
my backbone was sitting in the next room. "Well,
I won't keep quiet. The damned thing is too wrong
in principle. I won't be hushed up—elected or not
elected: I'll just be damned if I will."

"Oh, Cap'n Bob, sir—don't," begged Mr. Welch,
his voice unsteady with emotion. "I can't bear to see

you licked. The likes o' you should be rich and powerful. I don't want to see you whipped—not now—at your age."

"I am rich and powerful," laughed my father in one of his quick, gay changes of mood; "no matter how much money a man has he can't eat any more than I do. He couldn't have a better digestion or more friends. He couldn't enjoy God's fresh air and sunshine more than I do. He couldn't sleep more soundly—and that is *powerful* unusual for anyone my age."

"Those things are enough for a poor blacksmith like me," replied Mr. Welch, still grave in spite of Father's levity, "and I count myself happy to have them. But you should have more, Cap'n Bob, you—you are an aristocrat," said Mr. Welch doggedly. "A man like you should never know defeat."

My father got up from his chair. He walked across the room and laid his hand affectionately upon Mr. Welch's shoulder.

"My dear Tom," he said warmly, "you and your family have followed the same honorable calling for generations. You have a sense of responsibility toward your work and a sense of responsibility toward your fellowman. You are an aristocrat, Tom. There is no other aristocracy that amounts to a damn. You would not put inferior metal into your work. Your father would not have done it. Your

268

grandfather would not have done it. You don't want me to do it, do you, Tom? You don't want to muzzle your old friend. I have always fought what I thought was wrong. I believe people expect that of me. I expect it of myself. And I will continue to fight as hard as I can."

And Father did continue to give the Ku Klux a fit. And much to everybody's surprise, he was elected in 1925.

But now it was 1929. And Father was older still. And as the time for the candidates to announce themselves drew near, my mother again began to urge Father to retire.

"Really," said my mother, "I don't believe you will be satisfied until you have had that office for a hundred years. I believe that Gabriel will have to come and pull you out on Judgment Day," she laughed in exasperation.

"Well, and why not?" replied my father. He saw no reason for him to retire just because he had held a position for thirty-four years. Length of time had nothing to do with it. He was still hale and hearty. Of course he would stand for reelection.

Mother, however, saw that Father was not so hale and hearty as he claimed to be. It wasn't that Father had any actual symptoms. It was just that his appearance had changed. He had a sort of transparent look that some old people get—it was almost ethereal. Oddly, my father, who had always belonged very much to this world, suddenly seemed not to belong here at all. Sometimes when I looked at him, I had a feeling that he might float into space—clear, transparent skin, a halo of soft cloud-white hair, eyes which had not lost any of their penetration and yet, in some intangible way, were soft with a look of expectancy. I say this is a look that some old people get. And yet what I am really trying to describe is a look of ageless, timeless youth; the mystic look of the very young and innocent and of the very old and wise. They seem to have some touch with a place we do not know. I was accustomed to associate this look with old people of a deeply spiritual nature. I was surprised to see this look on Father's face, and yet there it was.

My mother was worried about this vague change in Father. She thought the excitement of running for office would be bad for him and, when two young and vigorous candidates came out against Father, my mother's worry became alarm. Since Father would not withdraw from the field, she tried to prevail upon him to go to our family physician and have a thorough physical examination before the fight began. But Father would not be persuaded into that either. Finally my mother gave up trying to induce him to go to the doctor and she went herself.

Of course our doctor could not diagnose Father from Mother's indefinable apprehensions concerning him. He told my mother she must manage some way to make Father come himself.

"Oh, I have tried every way," replied my mother. "He will not come. He has never had a doctor in his life; I have never known him to be sick. He thinks if people keep clean and take a lot of exercise they don't need doctors. There is no way to make Mr. Yancey come here. Couldn't you just give me a few suggestions that you think might be useful?"

So then Dr. Dudley was persuaded to give my mother a few general suggestions. He said that the most probable ailments of people Father's age were high blood pressure and bad hearts. In the first case, my father's diet should be watched. In either case he should avoid excitement, and of course he should cut down on tobacco.

"Oh—oh," said my mother in distress, "he lives on excitement. He can make something exciting out of the most trivial incident—and he eats more than any two people I ever saw—yet he is not overweight, you know—he has never been overweight. Oh—I am afraid I can't do much with him—he would never do without his pipe, I am sure——"

Nevertheless, when my mother came home from her visit to Dr. Dudley, she gave Father quite a lecture on high blood pressure and heart ailments.

"Bosh!" said my father, "I am not conscious that I *have* a heart or such a thing as blood pressure. I never interfere with their business, and I expect them to show me the same consideration."

"How absurd!" my mother returned. "Every intelligent person should go to a doctor and get checked over once in a while. You know perfectly well, whether you will admit it or not, that doctors nowadays know how to prolong a person's life by years."

"Yes, by years in bed; without any tobacco," scoffed Father, "—or existing on the diet of a suckling pig. I don't call that prolonging life. It is merely prolonging death. And furthermore, it doesn't concern me—for nothing is the matter with me except in your imagination."

My mother gave it up. She could not make Father stop eating "red" meat. She could not make him cut down on tobacco. And excitement was the very breath of his nostrils.

The campaign for the office of Commonwealth's Attorney was by now well under way. This gave my mother an opportunity to try her last hope. She appealed to Mr. Welch.

Mr. Welch usually came to our house at some time during the course of every month. He would pull a chair up to Father's secretary and together they would go over the progress of certain phases of the campaign that Mr. Welch was working on. So once, when Mr. Welch had finished his business with Father and was preparing to leave, my mother got him out of Father's hearing by pretending to ask his advice about the repair of an iron railing on the side porch. Then she urged upon Mr. Welch that he must use every bit of the influence he had with Father to make him retire from this race.

"Mr. Welch," said my mother, "I don't like the way Mr. Yancey looks. He isn't well. He is no match for two vigorous young men. He will be badly defeated and that will break his heart. You know how he is about his office. It is not that it is so wonderful to have. But, to him, it is a sort of symbol of his life which has been devoted to public service. It is better for him to get out than to be kicked out. I am afraid to think how he will be when he sees that people no longer want him. I have tried my best to stop him, Mr. Welch. Now you must try."

Mr. Welch stood towering like a great monolith above my mother. He was holding his hat in one enormous hand and with the other he turned it around and around; but he looked at my mother with steady eyes.

"No'm, Mrs. Yancey," he answered simply, "I can't try. He beat the Ku Klux. He may be a match for two young men. And if he ain't—well, ma'am,

I think it will be better for Cap'n Bob to go through with it and to get beat bad than to back down. The ole Cap'n, ma'am—he don't know how to retire."

After that my mother made no further attempt to induce my father to give up the fight. And my mother's predictions proved to be right. Father was no match for two vigorous young men. My father lost his election.

There it was, at last; and we had to face it. It did not take any extraordinary insight on the part of any one of us to guess that Father had never dreamed he could be beaten. We all knew he felt that the office of State's Attorney belonged exclusively to him. So much so, that my mother had often accused him of considering the position hereditary. The mere routine of running for office had always been just a kind of byplay with Father. The office belonged to him and the fight for reelection was simply a little excitement that went along with it; a recurrent opportunity for everyone to show how much they thought of him. But now it was over. And anyone could see that it was over for good.

And so it was a very troubled group that gathered at the breakfast table the morning after the votes had been counted. We dreaded the sound of Father's footsteps descending the stairs—lagging and frustrated. We hated the thought of facing Father—an old man crushed and broken. We all felt like running away and hiding before he should come down to breakfast.

And then, at last, we heard Father on the stairway. His footsteps were not lagging and frustrated. No—Father was whistling "La Paloma" and his feet accompanied with a spirited tattoo. And now he came into the room.

"Well!" said my Father, with a comical lilt to his voice, "instead of being elected I find myself rejected and all the house dejected," and he looked around at us all with such an artless, small-boy expression that nobody could help laughing at his silly rhyme.

"You are the biggest goose that ever lived," declared my mother, halfway between tears and laughter.

But Father's foolishness had cleared the atmosphere, and our uneasiness did not return until he left to walk, as usual, to his office. Then our thoughts followed him. Even as he closed the front door we fancied him having to meet people all day, hurt at receiving their sympathy and yet unable to avoid them.

"Poor old man!" said my mother as we crowded to the window to watch Father take his accustomed course across the street and down past the fire station.

When his good friends, the firemen, saw him

coming they looked as if they too wanted to run away and hide. As they sat in their accustomed places along the fence, one got very much preoccupied with his shoe laces, one reached into his pocket for a cigarette and then became quite busy with his lighter, another held the morning paper up in front of his face. The others just sat sadly hanging their heads and pretending not to see my father coming.

But Father would not have it so. He knew they were aware of him in spite of their pretense and, walking straight into their midst, he anticipated their embarrassment:

"Well, boys!" he said, "those fellows certainly gave us one hell of a licking!" and his laugh rang out warm, free and inclusive. All the firemen joined in with the loud laughter of relief; and on the moment, they were out of their seats, slapping Father on the back, shaking his hand, joking, laughing, teasing.

"Poor old man!" my mother repeated, again halfway between laughing and weeping.

"Poor old man? Rats!" snapped someone at the window. "The old boy's got everything under control. He can take it! Just watch him go to town!"

We saw Father's chin go up—and he was smiling. With the laughing voices of the firemen still sounding behind him, he passed on down the street,

stepping along as blithely as a robin in the spring-
time.

*   *   *   *   *

Father did not live long after that. He had a sudden heart attack and went before anyone realized
what was happening. My younger sister was with
him at the time. She did not know how ill Father
was, but she did manage to persuade him to lie
down on his bed.

"I will just lie here for a few minutes," Father
had insisted. "—I will stay here a little while, just
to please you—don't leave me, little lady. I love to
watch your bright young face. Two things in this
world I have always loved—a bright young face
and—walking in the sunshine——"

These were the last words Father spoke.